Fostering Now

Current law including regulations, guidance and standards (England)

Fergus Smith and Chris Brann
with Alexandra Conroy Harris

British Association for Adoption & Fostering
(BAAF)
Saffron House
6–10 Kirby Street
London EC1N 8TS
www.baaf.org.uk

Charity registration 275689 (England and Wales)
and SC039337 (Scotland)

British Library Cataloguing in Publication Data
A catalogue recored for this book is available
from the British Library

ISBN 978 1 907585 28 9

Designed by Andrew Haig & Associates
Typeset by Avon DataSet Ltd, Bidford on Avon
Printed in Great Britain by the Lavenham Press

BAAF is the leading UK-wide membership
organisation for all those concerned with
adoption, fostering and child care issues.

Contents

Notes about the authors

Fergus Smith is the Director of Children Act Enterprises Ltd (www.caeuk.org), an independent social work consultancy which undertakes research, consultancy, training and independent investigation. Fergus is also the author of over a dozen pocket-sized guides to family and criminal law written in consultation with acknowledged experts in their field.

Chris Brann is an independent child care consultant and chair of adoption panels, and an associate consultant with CAE. Chris has extensive practice and management experience of adoption, fostering and planning for looked after children, and was the consultant for CAE's guide to the LAC information and planning system.

Alexandra Conroy Harris is BAAF's Legal Consultant. She is a barrister with over twenty years' experience of representing parents, children and local authorities in care and adoption proceedings. She spent nine years as a senior social services lawyer for a London borough, during which she was a committed user of this guide's previous edition. She has worked for BAAF since 2008 and produces the Legal Notes for the *Adoption & Fostering* journal.

Note to this edition

This 2011 edition of *Fostering Now* has been comprehensively revised and updated in line with recent legislative changes. The principal authors of the first edition were Fergus Smith and Chris Brann, with Deborah Cullen and Mary Lane. This second edition has been updated throughout by Alexandra Conroy Harris, BAAF's Legal Consultant.

Abbreviations

Legislation

ACA 2002: Adoption & Children Act 2002
CA 1989: Children Act 1989
CPPR 2010: Care Planning, Placement & Case Review (England) Regulations 2010
CSA 2000: Care Standards Act 2000
CYPA 1969: Children & Young Persons Act 1969
FSR 2011: Fostering Services (England) Regulations 2011
PA 1997: Police Act 1997

Organisations

CAFCASS: Children and Families Courts Advisory and Support Service
CI: Her Majesty's Chief Inspector of Schools, Children's Services and Skills
CRB: Criminal Records Bureau
FSP: Fostering service provider
IFA: Independent fostering agency
IFP: Independent fostering provider
LA: Local authority
NCSC: National Care Standards Commission
OFSTED: the Office for Standards in Education, Children's Services and Skills

Introduction

This guide is designed for use in England by those who provide or work in fostering services and agencies, foster carers and young persons in foster care.

Regulations and national minimum standards in Wales are comparable but not identical to those applicable to England. The registration body for Wales is the National Assembly.

This guide is intended to facilitate understanding of the obligations and expectations of legislation – Care Standards Act 2000 (CSA 2000), Children Act 1989 (CA 1989), the Fostering Services (England) Regulations 2011 (FSR 2011), and other relevant regulations and the national minimum standards for fostering.

The CSA 2000 created the National Care Standards Commission (NCSC), an independent non-departmental body responsible for regulation of a range of health and care services, including foster care of children.

With effect from 1 April 2007, The Office for Standards in Education, Children's Services and Skills (OFSTED) took over responsibility for the inspection and regulation of fostering services.

OFSTED assesses, on the basis of the FSR 2011 (compliance with which is mandatory), and achievement of national minimum standards (issued by the Secretary of State under section 23(1) CSA 2000), whether services being provided by a local authority, an independent fostering provider or a voluntary organisation are satisfactory.

When OFSTED makes any decision about registration, cancellation, variation or imposition of conditions, it must take the national minimum standards as well as any other factors considered reasonable and relevant, into account.

With respect to independent fostering providers and voluntary organisations, if a regulation is breached and an offence committed, providers will be given a notice setting out:

- regulation breached
- how the service is considered deficient
- what must be done to remedy the deficiency
- a timescale within which the deficiency must be remedied.

- If the deficiency is not remedied, a prosecution may follow.

- In the case of a local authority service, the enforcement route is via the Secretary of State to whom OFSTED will report a substantial failure to meet a regulation. If there is a failure which is not substantial, OFSTED may serve an enforcement notice under section 47(5) CSA 2000.

Terms used in this guide

- We have used the term 'foster parent' throughout the book (except for the section on national minimum standards) as this reflects the term used in primary and subordinate legislation. The term 'foster carer' has been used in the section on national minimum standards, as this reflects the term used.

- We have used the term 'independent fostering agency', as well as the term 'independent fostering provider', as both are used in primary and subordinate legislation as well as in the standards.

Part I

Definitions

Definitions

Child

- A person aged less than 18 years old.

- Parental responsibility is all the rights, duties and responsibilities that by law a parent has in relation to a child. Includes the right to decide where a child lives, their names, medical consents, how she/he is educated, and for parents and legal guardians only, to give or withhold agreement to the making of an adoption order.

Fostering service [reg.2 FSR 2011]

- A fostering service means:
    - a fostering agency as defined in section 4(4) CSA 2000 i.e. a private or voluntary organisation that carries out fostering functions of a local authority or
    - a local authority fostering service.

- An 'independent fostering agency' (or 'provider') is one falling within the definition of section 4(4)(a) CSA 2000 i.e. discharging functions of local authorities in connection with placing of children with foster parents.

- Area authority is the local authority in whose area the foster parent lives, if that is different from the responsible authority for the child.

- Responsible authority means, in relation to a child, the local authority (or voluntary organisation) responsible for the child's placement.

Fostering service provider

- A fostering service provider means:

- in relation to an independent fostering agency, the registered person
- in relation to a local authority fostering service, a local authority.

Looked after children [s.22 CA 1989]

- A child who is 'looked after' by a local authority may be 'accommodated', 'in care', 'remanded/detained' or 'placed for adoption'.

- **'Accommodated' children [s.20 CA 1989]**
  Accommodation of a child is a voluntary legal arrangement between parents or others with parental responsibility for a child and the local authority. The local authority does not acquire parental responsibility. A child can be removed from accommodation, including a foster home, by a parent or other person with parental responsibility at any time, unless the local authority is granted an Emergency Protection Order, or Interim Care Order, entitling it to prevent removal.

- **Children 'in care' [ss.38 & 31 CA 1989]**
  A child 'in care' means that a court has granted an Interim Care Order or Care Order to the local authority, which gives it parental responsibility, shared with parents who have parental responsibility, and the legal entitlement to limit the exercise of parental responsibility by the parents, including the right of the local authority to prevent the child's removal from a foster home.

- **'Detained' children**
  A local authority has the legal duty to accommodate children and young persons remanded to their care, but does not gain parental responsibility.

- **Children 'placed for adoption' [s.18 ACA 2002]**
  When a placement order is made, parental responsibility for the child is shared between the local authority and the parents in the same way as under a Care Order. When a child is placed with prospective adopters parental responsibility is also given to them, subject to any restrictions determined by the LA [s.25 ACA 2002].

Parental responsibility and foster parents

- Foster parents do not acquire parental responsibility for the children placed with them by a responsible authority.

- A Residence Order [s.8 CA 1989] made in favour of foster parents discharges a Care Order, and parental responsibility is then shared with parents and any others with parental responsibility, but the Residence Order determines that the child lives with the foster parents.

  Local authority foster parents cannot apply for a Residence Order until the child has lived with them for one year unless they are relatives of the child, or the local authority supports an earlier application [s.9(3) CA 1989].

- A Special Guardianship Order [s.14A CA 1989] discharges a Care Order and gives parental responsibility to the Special Guardian. The Special Guardian can exercise their parental responsibility to override the parental responsibility held by any other person.

- Local authority foster parents cannot apply for a Special Guardianship Order until the child has lived with them for one year unless the local authority supports an earlier application [ss.9(3) & 14A(5) CA 1989].

- An Adoption Order [s.46 ACA 2002] discharges a Care Order or a Placement for Adoption Order, and vests parental responsibility solely in the adopter/s. Local authority foster parents may adopt children in their care either by being approved as prospective adopters and being matched with the children or by making a private application to adopt them. Local authority foster parents cannot apply privately for an Adoption Order until the child has lived with them for one year unless the court gives leave for an earlier application [ss.42(4) & 42(6) ACA 2002). A private Adoption Order cannot be granted unless the foster parents have, three months prior to making their application, given notice to the local authority of their intention to apply for an Adoption Order [s.44 ACA 2002].

Parent [reg.2 FSR 2011]

- A parent, in relation to a child, includes any person who has parental responsibility for her/him.

Registered manager [reg.2 FSR 2011]

- The registered manager means the person who is registered under Part II CSA 2000 as the manager of the fostering agency.

Registered person [reg.2 FSR 2011]

- The registered person means the person who is the registered provider or the registered manager of the fostering agency.

Registered provider [reg.2 FSR 2011]

- The registered provider means the person who is registered under Part II of the CSA 2000 as the person carrying on the fostering agency.

  In the case of a voluntary organisation which places children with foster parents under section 59(1) CA 1989, section 121(4) CSA 2000 defines the 'person carrying on a fostering agency' as the voluntary organisation itself.

Legal routes into foster care

Accommodating a child [s.20 CA 1989]

- One of the family support services the local authority must provide is that of 'accommodating' (in family or residential settings) anyone under 18 'in need' who requires it as a result of:

  - there being no person with parental responsibility for her/him
  - she/he being lost or having been abandoned or

- the person who has been caring for her/him being prevented temporarily or permanently (for whatever reason) from providing suitable care/accommodation.

- This service is a voluntary arrangement and the local authority does not gain parental responsibility.

- A person with parental responsibility has the right to remove a child from such an arrangement [s.20(8) CA 1989] but:

  - a holder of a Residence Order or Special Guardianship Order could authorise the retention of a child in accommodation in spite of parent's wishes to remove [s.20(9) CA 1989]
  - a young person of 16 or 17 could overrule their parent's wishes to remove them [s.20(11) CA 1989].

- Anyone who does not have parental responsibility for a child but does have actual care of her/him may do what is reasonable in the circumstances to safeguard and promote the child's welfare [s.3(5) CA 1989].

- If there is a risk of significant harm, or actual significant harm to a child, an Emergency Protection Order may be applied for by anyone. This will allow the holder of the EPO to prevent the child's removal from accommodation [s.44 CA 1989].

Accommodating a 16- or 17-year-old [s.20(3) CA 1989]

- A local authority must provide accommodation to a young person in the above age group if:

  - she/he is 'in need' and her/his welfare would otherwise be 'seriously prejudiced'.

Other obligations to accommodate [ss.21(1), (2) & 33(1) CA 1989]

- When asked, the local authority must 'accommodate' (provide a home for) children and young persons:

- removed from home on an Emergency Protection Order, Child Assessment Order or an Interim Care Order
- in police protection
- remanded by a court
- detained under the Police & Criminal Evidence Act 1984
- the subject of a youth rehabilitation order with fostering or a local authority residence requirement [s.1 Criminal Justice and Immigration Act 2008]
- on a Supervision Order with residence requirements [s.12AA Children & Young Persons Act 1969 (CYPA 1969)].

Care proceedings [ss.31 & 38 CA 1989]

- A court may make an interim or a full Care Order if it is satisfied that a child is suffering, or is likely to suffer, significant harm, and that this is attributable to:
  - the care being given the child, or likely to be given if an order is not made, not being what it would be reasonable to expect a parent to provide, or
  - the child being beyond parental control.
- An interim or full Care Order means the child is 'in care'. Either order provides the local authority with parental responsibility but does not remove parents' parental responsibility.

Local authority general duties towards looked after children [ss.22, 22C, 23, 24 & Sch.2 CA 1989]

- Safeguard and promote their welfare and make reasonable efforts to allow the child access to ordinary services as though still at home.

- Endeavour, unless not reasonably practicable or consistent with a child's welfare, to promote contact between the child and:
  - parents, and others with parental responsibility
  - relatives, friends or persons connected with her/him (see 'Contact for children in foster care' p.25).
- Take reasonable steps to keep parents and those with parental responsibility informed of the child's location, unless to do so would not be in the interests of the child 'in care' [Sch.2 para.15 CA 1989].
- Before making any decision, ascertain the wishes/feelings of the:
  - child
  - parent/s and any others who have parental responsibility and relevant others.
- Give due consideration to these views (having regard in the case of the child to level of understanding, religion, racial origin, cultural and linguistic background).
- A local authority may act contrary to the above in order to protect the public from serious injury [s.22 CA 1989].

Duty to place a looked after child with family or friends

- Unless it is not reasonably practicable or consistent with welfare, place a child with:
  - parents
  - someone else who has parental responsibility
  - (for a child 'in care') any previous Residence Order holder.

If the LA is unable to place with any of the above, the child should be placed with a relative, friend or other person connected with her/him who is also an LA foster parent in preference to stranger foster carers, placement in a children's home or other arrangement.

- As far as reasonably practicable, ensure placement is near home, within the LA's area, does not disrupt the child's education and that looked after siblings are placed together [s.22C CA 1989].

Additional duties towards children with disabilities

- Work with children who have disabilities should be based on the principles that:
  - they are children first and their disabilities are a secondary, albeit significant issue
  - the aim should be to promote access to the same range of services for all.
- Local authorities:
  - must, so far as is practical, when they provide accommodation for a child with disabilities, ensure that the accommodation is suitable for her/his needs [s.22C(8)(d) CA 1989].

Discharge of local authority fostering duties by independent fostering agencies (IFAs) [reg.26 CPPR 2010]

- A local authority (LA) may make arrangements for its fostering services duties under regulations 14(3) CPPR 2010 (terminating placement where the child is at risk) and 22 CPPR 2010 (making placements with foster parents) to be discharged on its behalf by a registered person (in an IFA) subject to the following conditions:
- No arrangement to delegate the LA's fostering duties to an IFA can be made until the LA and IFA (registered person) have entered into a written agreement, which sets out:

- the services to be provided by the IFA to the LA
- the arrangements for the selection by the LA of particular foster parents from those approved by the IFA
- a requirement for the IFA to submit reports to the LA on any placement as may be required by the LA
- the arrangements for termination of the agreement.

Arrangements with respect to a particular child

- The local authority and IFA must enter into an agreement which sets out:
  - details of the particular foster parent with whom the child is to be placed
  - details of any services the child is to receive and whether they are to be provided by the LA or the IFA
  - the terms (including as to payment) of the proposed foster placement agreement
  - the arrangements for record keeping about the child, and for return of records at the end of the placement
  - a requirement for the IFA to notify the LA immediately in the event of any concerns about the placement
  - whether, and on what basis, other children may be placed with the foster parent [reg.26 & Sch.5 CPPR 2010].
- IFA approved foster parents come within the definition of local authority foster parents [s.22C(12) CA 1989].

Making placements – Duties of the 'responsible authority' (local authority or voluntary organisation)

- National Minimum Fostering Standards 1 to 12 apply, as does standard 15 – 'Matching the child with a placement that meets their assessed needs'.

Usual fostering limit [Sch.7 paras (2) to (5) CA 1989]

- A person may not foster more than three children, unless the children concerned are all siblings with respect to each other.

- The usual fostering limit may be exceeded if the local authority for the area where the foster parent resides, exempts the foster carer from this restriction for specific children, taking into account the considerations listed in paragraph 4(2) of Schedule 7.

- Foster parents can complain about the local authority's decision in respect of this exemption under regulation 23 of the Children Act 1989 Representations Procedure (England) Regulations 2006.

Types of foster placements

- Placements with foster parents may include:

  - **planned temporary or permanent placements** with approved foster parents, including relatives or friends of the child, and 'concurrent' placements (see below)

  - **emergency or immediate placements** with approved foster parents, or 'connected people' who have been temporarily approved (see below)

  - **a series of short-term placements with the same approved foster parents.**

- **A 'concurrent' placement** is where a child is placed with a plan that his/her approved foster parent(s) are involved in assessment and efforts by the local authority to secure the child's return to parents, and are also approved adoptive parent(s) who may apply to adopt the child if the reunification with parent(s) does not succeed.

- A 'connected person' is a relative, friend or other person connected to the child who may be approved as a foster carer for a period of up to 16 weeks to allow placement of the child before full assessment of the connected person as a foster carer [reg.24 CPPR 2010].

Advance notification of placements [regs.9(1)(b) & 13 CPPR 2010, & ss.22(4) & 61(2) CA 1989]

- Unless it is not reasonably practicable, the responsible authority (see definitions) must provide advance written notification of the arrangements to place a child in foster care to:

  - the child, depending on his/her age and understanding
  - parents and any other person who has parental responsibility for the child
  - the Primary Care Trust where the child is to be living, and from where she/he is to be placed
  - the school or other place of education or training, or a person providing education or training, to the child
  - the child's registered medical practitioner, and the GP with whom the child is to become registered
  - any person who was caring for the child immediately before the placement
  - any person in whose favour there was a contact order – section 8 CA 1989 – or who has contact with a child 'in care' – section 34 CA 1989
  - the Independent Reviewing Officer for the child.

- If the placement is made in an emergency, written notification as above must be given within five working days of the start of the placement.

Planned placements with approved foster parents – temporary, permanent or concurrent [reg.22 FSR 2011]

- Except in the case of an emergency or immediate placement, the responsible authority may only place a child with a foster parent if:

  - the foster parent is approved
    - by the responsible authority proposing to make the placement

- by another fostering service provider if both the IFP and any LA responsible for a child already placed with that foster carer consent to the placement

- the terms of her/his approval are consistent with the proposed placement
- she/he has entered into a foster care agreement in accordance with regulation 28(5)(b) FSR 2011.

A series of short-term placements with the same approved foster parent(s) [reg.48 CPPR 2010]

- Regulation 48 applies where a responsible authority has arranged to place a child in a series of short-term placements with the same foster parent(s) and the arrangement is such that:

  - the child is not in care
  - at the end of each placement the child returns to the care of a parent or a person with parental responsibility
  - no single placement is to last for more than 17 days, and
  - the total duration of the placements is not to exceed 75 days in any period of 12 months.

Emergency placements by local authorities [reg.23 CPPR 2010]

- Where a child is to be placed in an emergency, a local authority may place the child with any approved foster parent for no longer than six working days.

  - if the foster carer's terms of approval are inconsistent with the placement, the LA must terminate the placement after six working days unless the terms of approval have been amended. It is not possible to amend terms of approval within six days, as variation can only be made through a review and the fostering service provider's decision cannot be made until the 28-day period allowed for representations has expired [reg.28(9) FSR 2011]. (See DfE website http://media.education.gov.uk/assets/files/pdf/f/faqs%20on%20changing%20terms%20of%20approval.pdf.)

Temporary approval of relatives and friends carers [reg.24 CPPR 2010]

- Where a local authority is satisfied that the most appropriate placement for a child is with a friend, relative or other connected person and that it is necessary to place the child before that person could be approved as a foster carer in accordance with the FSR 2011, they may approve that connected person as a foster carer for a temporary period not exceeding 16 weeks, but only after:
  - assessing the suitability of the connected person to care for the child, including:
    - their accommodation, neighbourhood and community
    - all adult members of their household
    - their relationship with the child
    - their physical, emotional and mental health
    - their family history and relationships
    - their capacity to care for children and for the particular child
    - any criminal record [reg.24 & Sch. 4 CPPR 2010]
  - considering whether in all the circumstances, including services to be provided, the arrangements will safeguard and promote the child's welfare and meet his/her needs
  - making immediate arrangements for the connected person to be assessed as a foster carer under the FSR 2011 before the temporary period of approval expires.
- If the 16-week period is likely to expire before the full assessment has been completed, the LA may extend the temporary approval for a further period

of up to eight weeks, but may only do so once, after considering whether the placement is still the most appropriate placement available for the child, seeking the views of the fostering panel and informing the IRO.

- If the connected person is not approved as a foster carer and makes an application to the Independent Review Mechanism, the LA may extend the temporary approval until the outcome of the review is known.

- Any decision to extend temporary approval must be approved by a nominated officer, a senior member of the LA's staff identified in writing by the Director of Children's Services.

Kinship foster care – placements of looked after children with relatives and friends without parental responsibility [s.22C(6)(a) CA 1989]

- All fostering standards apply. Standard 30 is specifically about family and friends foster carers.

- An accommodated child may not be placed with a friend or relative who does not have parental responsibility for the child, unless that relative or person has been approved as a foster parent under regulation 27 FSR 2011 or regulation 24 CPPR 2010. The alternative would be for the child to cease being accommodated, and to live with the person concerned with the agreement of a parent with parental responsibility (subject to possible private fostering assessment and monitoring).

- A child 'in care' may only be placed with a relative or friend if either:

  - they are a parent, have parental responsibility for the child, or had a Residence Order in respect of the child immediately before the Care Order was made, in which case the child may be placed pursuant to regulations 15–20 CPPR 2010 or

  - they have been approved as foster parents, temporarily under regulation

24 CPPR 2010, or fully under regulation 27 FSR 2011. (*Re W and X [Wardship: Relatives rejected as Foster Carers]* [2004] 1 FLR 415)

Whilst a court may find it to be in the best interests of children to be made the subject of Care Orders and placed with relatives/friends, a court is unable to make Care Orders and endorse a care plan for the children to be placed with friends/relatives, if the local authority does not find them suitable for approval as foster carers. The court may only make such a placement by making the child a ward of court.

- All relatives and other persons approved under regulations 27 FSR 2011 or 24 CPPR 2010 are LA foster parents, and therefore subject to the same law, regulations and guidance as any other LA foster parents.

  Placements of children 'in care' with their parents or other persons who have or had parental responsibility for them are under regulations 15–20 of the CPPR 2010, and are not within the scope of this publication.

Placements outside the area [reg.11 FSR 2011]

- A decision to place a child outside the area of the responsible authority must be taken by a nominated officer, who must be satisfied that the child's wishes and feelings have been given due consideration and that the placement is the most appropriate available.

  - unless the child is being placed with a connected person or a foster carer approved by the responsible authority, the child's relatives and IRO must be consulted and the LA for the area be notified

  - if the placement is made in an emergency the IRO and area authority must be informed and the child's relatives consulted within five working days of the decision.

Placements outside England [reg.12 CPPR 2010]

- Where a responsible authority makes arrangements to place a child outside England it shall ensure, so far as is reasonably practicable, that the requirements that would have applied under the regulations, had the child been placed in England, are complied with.

- In the case of a placement by a local authority of a child 'in care' outside England or Wales, the above is subject to the provisions of paragraph 19 of Schedule 2 to CA 1989 (arrangements to assist children 'in care' to live abroad).

Placement plan agreements – all placements except emergency/ immediate [reg.9(3) CPPR 2010]

- Before making any foster care placement (other than an emergency or immediate placement), the responsible authority shall prepare a placement plan for the child, which covers the matters specified in Schedule 2, which must be agreed with and signed by the foster carer. If it is not reasonably practicable to prepare the plan before placement, it must be done within five working days of the start of the placement.

Schedule 2 – Matters dealt with in the placement plan

- A statement by the responsible authority setting out how the placement will contribute to meeting the child's needs, including:
    - how the child will be cared for and his/her welfare safeguarded and promoted
    - the child's personal history, religious persuasion, and cultural and linguistic background and racial origin.
- The responsible authority's arrangements for the financial support of the child during the placement.

- The details of the child's registered GP and dentist.
- The arrangements for giving consent to the medical or dental examination or treatment of the child.
- The arrangements for the child's education or training.
- The circumstances in which it is necessary to obtain in advance the approval of the responsible authority for the child to take part in school trips, or stay overnight away from the foster parent's home.
- The arrangements for visits to the child by the person authorised by or on behalf of the responsible authority, and the frequency of visits and reviews.
- The arrangements for the child to have contact with her/his parents and any other specified persons, and details of any court order relating to contact.
- The obligation of the foster parent to comply with the terms of the foster care agreement made under regulation 27(5) FSR 2011.

Termination of placements [reg.14 CPPR 2010]

- A responsible authority may only terminate the placement of a child with a foster parent following a review of the child's case, unless the placement is terminated as a result of failure of the carer's approval as a foster parent [reg.14 CPPR 2010].

Duty of IFAs to secure welfare of children in foster care [reg.11 FSR 2011]

- The registered person in respect of an IFA shall ensure that:
  - the welfare of children placed or to be placed with foster parents is safeguarded and promoted at all times, and

- before making any decision affecting a child placed or to be placed with foster parents, due consideration is given to:
  - the child's wishes and feelings in the light of her/his age and understanding, and
  - her/his religious persuasion, racial origin and cultural and linguistic background.

Arrangements by all fostering service providers for the protection of children in foster care [reg.12(1) FSR 2011]

- The fostering service provider shall prepare and implement a written policy which:
  - is intended to safeguard children placed with foster parents from abuse or neglect
  - includes a statement of measures to be taken to safeguard any child before making a parent and child placement
  - sets out the procedure to be followed in the event of any allegation of abuse or neglect.
- This procedure shall provide in particular for:
  - liaison and co-operation with any LA which is, or may be, making child protection enquiries in relation to any child placed by the fostering service provider*
  - the prompt referral to the area authority of any allegation of abuse or neglect affecting any child placed by the fostering service provider
  - notification of the instigation and outcome of any child protection enquiries involving a child placed by the fostering service provider, to the Chief Inspector (OFSTED) *
  - written records to be kept of any allegation of abuse or neglect, and of the action taken in response

- consideration to be given to the measures which may be necessary to protect children placed with foster parents following an allegation of abuse or neglect, and
- arrangements to be made for persons working for the purposes of a fostering service, foster parents and children placed by the fostering service, to have the address, email address and telephone number of
  - the area authority and
  - the Chief Inspector (OFSTED)

  in order to report any concern about child welfare or safety.

- The sub-paragraphs above marked * do not apply to a local authority fostering service.
- In this regulation, 'child protection enquiries' means any enquiries carried out by an LA in the exercise of any of its functions conferred by or under the Children Act 1989 relating to the protection of children.

Behaviour management [reg.13(1) & (2) FSR 2011]

- The fostering service provider must prepare and implement a written policy on acceptable measures of control, restraint and discipline of children placed with foster parents.
- The fostering service provider must take all reasonable steps to ensure that:
  - no form of corporal punishment is used on any child placed with a foster parent
  - no child placed with foster parents is subject to any measure of control, restraint or discipline which is excessive or unreasonable, and
  - restraint is used on a child only where it is necessary to prevent injury to the child or other persons or likely serious damage to property.

Child missing from foster parent's home [reg.13(3) FSR 2011]

- The fostering service provider must prepare and implement a written procedure to be followed if a child is missing from a foster parent's home without permission.

Guidance on overnight stays (Fostering Services 2011 Statutory Guidance para 3.17)

- There is no statutory duty for CRB checks to be carried out on the people with whom the looked after child stays.

- Responsibility for decisions on overnight stays should be delegated to foster carers, with details included in the placement agreement as stated in Schedule 2 of the FSR 2011.

- Normally, looked after children should be granted the same permissions to take part in acceptable age-appropriate peer activities as would reasonably be granted by the parents of their peers. However, where exceptional circumstances mean that this is not possible, the decision should be based on clear reasons and stated in the child's care plan, and where practicable the child's views and feelings should be taken into account.

- Local authorities are expected to review their policies and practices in accordance with this guidance, and to ensure that foster carers, staff, children and young people are aware of the situation.

Health and education of children in foster care [regs.15 & 16 FSR 2011, regs.5 & 7 CPPR 2010]

- National minimum standard 6 applies: 'Children's physical, emotional and social development needs are promoted.'

Health assessments before placement in foster care [reg.7 CPPR 2010]

A responsible authority shall:

- before first placing a child, or if that is not reasonably practicable, before the first review of the child's case, make arrangements for a registered medical practitioner to carry out an assessment of the child's state of health and provide a written report of the assessment addressing the matters specified in Paragraph 1 of Schedule 1

  (This does not apply if the child, being of sufficient understanding to do so, refuses to consent to the assessment.)

  (The above does not apply if, within a period of three months immediately preceding the placement, an assessment of the child's health has been carried out and a written report obtained that meets the requirements of that paragraph.)

- the child's care plan must include the arrangements made by the responsible authority to meet the child's health needs ('the health plan').

▪ A responsible authority must take all reasonable steps to ensure that each child is provided with appropriate health care services, in accordance with the health plan, including

  - medical and dental care and treatment and
  - advice and guidance on health, personal care and health promotion issues.

▪ Information to be included in the health plan [Sch.1 CPPR 2010]:

  - the child's state of health including her/his physical, emotional and mental health
  - the child's health history including, as far as practicable, her/his family health history
  - the effect of the child's health and health history on her/his development
  - existing arrangements for the child's medical and dental care including:

  - routine general health checks, including dental checks
  - treatment and monitoring of identified health needs
  - preventive measures, such as vaccination and immunisation, and screening for vision and hearing
  - advice and guidance on promoting health and personal care
- any planned changes to existing arrangements
- the role of the person caring for the child in promoting her/his health.

Health in foster care [reg.15 FSR 2011]

- The fostering service provider must promote the health and development of children placed with foster parents.
- In particular, the fostering service provider must ensure that:
  - each child is registered with a GP
  - each child has access to such medical, dental, nursing, psychological and psychiatric advice, treatment and other services as she/he may require
  - each child is provided with such individual support, aids and equipment which she/he may require as a result of any particular health needs or disability she/he may have, and
  - each child is provided with guidance, support and advice on health, personal care and health promotion issues appropriate to her/his needs and wishes.

Education, employment and leisure activities [reg.16 FSR 2011]

- The fostering service provider must promote the educational attainment of children placed with foster parents.
- In particular, the fostering service provider must:

- establish a procedure for monitoring the educational attainment, progress and school attendance of children placed with foster parents
- promote the regular school attendance and participation in school activities of school-aged children placed with foster parents, and
- provide foster parents with such information and assistance, including equipment, as may be necessary to meet the educational needs of children placed with them.

- The fostering service provider must ensure that any education it provides for any child placed with foster parents who is of compulsory school age but not attending school is efficient and suitable to the child's age, ability, aptitude, and any special educational needs she/he may have.

- The fostering service provider must ensure that foster parents promote the leisure interests of children placed with them.

- Where any child placed with foster parents is above compulsory school age, the fostering service provider must assist with the making of, and give effect to, the arrangements made for her/his education, training and employment.

Support, training and information for foster parents [reg.17 FSR 2011]

- The fostering service provider must provide foster parents with such training, advice, information and support (including support out of office hours) as appears necessary in the interests of children placed with them [reg.17(1)].

- The fostering service provider must take all reasonable steps to ensure that foster parents are familiar with and act in accordance with the policies established about child protection, behaviour management and children missing from a foster parent's home [reg.17(2)].

- The fostering service provider must ensure that in relation to any child placed or to be placed with her/him, a foster parent is given such information, which is kept up to date, as to enable her/him to provide appropriate care for the child.

- In particular, each foster parent must be provided with a copy of the most recent version of the child's care plan [reg.17(3)].

Contact for children in foster care

- National minimum standard 9 applies: 'Children are supported and encouraged to maintain and develop family contacts and friendships, subject to any limitations or provisions set out in their care plan and any court order.'

Promotion of contact by the fostering service [reg.14 FSR 2011]

- The fostering service provider must, subject to the provisions of the care plan and any court order relating to contact, promote contact between a child placed with a foster parent and her/his parents, relatives and friends unless such contact is not reasonably practicable or consistent with the child's welfare.

- Contact for children in foster care, as for all looked after children, is governed by the Children Act 1989, particularly Schedule 2, paragraph 15, and, for children in care, section 34.

Supervision of foster placements [regs.28–31 CPPR 2010]

- As part of their arrangements for supervising a child's welfare, the responsible authority must ensure that a child is visited:

  - whenever reasonably requested to do so by the child, the foster parent or the person responsible for the child's living arrangements
  - within one week of the start of any placement

- at intervals of not more than six weeks for the first year of any placement
- after the first year of placement
  - at intervals of not more than three months where the placement is intended to last until the child is 18
  - in any other case, at intervals of not more than six weeks.

Supervision of placements with connected people temporarily approved as foster carers [reg.28 CPPR 2010]

- The responsible authority must ensure that the child is visited at least once a week until the first review and thereafter at intervals of not more than four weeks.

Supervision of placements where another person is responsible for the child's living arrangements [reg.28 CPPR 2010]

- The responsible authority shall arrange for the child to be visited:
  - within a week of the start of, and of any change to, the child's living arrangements
  - at intervals of not more than six weeks during the first year
  - at intervals of not more than three months during any subsequent year.

Seeing the child alone and reports on supervision visits [reg.29 CPPR 2010]

- On each visit, the responsible authority's representative must speak to the child in private unless:
  - the child, being of sufficient age and understanding to do so, refuses
  - the representative considers it inappropriate to do so, having regard to the child's age and understanding, or
  - the representative is unable to do so.

Supervision of a series of short-term placements

- The responsible authority must ensure that the child is visited on days when the child is in placement, at regular intervals to be agreed with the IRO and the child's parents and in any event:
  - within three months of the start of the first placement or as soon as practicable thereafter
  - at intervals of not more that six months for as long as the short breaks continue [reg.48(3) CPPR 2010].

Reviews of foster placements [s.26 CA 1989 & regs.32–38 CPPR 2010]

- The responsible authority has a general duty to review a child's case. No significant changes to the child's care plan can be made unless the proposed change has been considered at a review, unless this is not reasonably practicable. There is nothing to prevent a review being held at the same time as any other review, assessment or consideration of the child's case.

Frequency of reviews [reg.33 CPPR 2010]

- The child's first review must be held within 20 working days of the date on which the child becomes looked after.
  - the second review must be carried out not more than three months after the first review
  - subsequent reviews must be carried out at intervals of not more than six months.
- An earlier review must be carried out if
  - the IRO requests it

- the responsible authority's representative carries out a visit and assesses that the child's welfare is not adequately safeguarded and promoted by the placement
- the child is detained under the Police and Criminal Evidence Act 1984, is remanded to LA accommodation or is accommodated under a youth rehabilitation order and a review would not otherwise occur before the child ceased to be so detained
- the child is detained in a secure training centre or young offender's institution and a review would not otherwise occur before the child ceased to be so detained
- the child is looked after by but not in the care of the responsible authority and the LA proposes to cease accommodating her/him, and the child will not be provided with accommodation by a parent or other person with parental responsibility.

Health reviews [reg.7 CPPR 2010]

- The responsible authority must make arrangements for the state of health of children who continue to be looked after/accommodated by it to be reviewed and for a written report addressing matters listed in paragraph 1 of Schedule 1 to be prepared at least:
  - once in every six month period for those under five years of age and
  - once in every 12 month period for those five years of age and over.
- The health review may be conducted by a registered medical practitioner or a registered nurse or midwife acting under her/his supervision.
- A child of sufficient age and understanding may refuse to consent to such an assessment.

Procedures for review, consultation, participation and notification [regs.34–38 CPPR 2010]

- Each responsible authority must prepare and implement a written policy on how they will review cases.

  A copy of the policy must be provided to:

  - the child, unless it is inappropriate to do so having regard to her/his age and understanding
  - the child's parent and any other person who has parental responsibility for the child
  - any other person whose views the responsible authority consider to be relevant.

Considerations to which the responsible authority must have regard [reg.35 & Sch. 7 CPPR 2010 & s.26 CA 1989]

- In reviewing a child's case, the responsible authority must consider:

  - the effect of any change in the child's circumstances since the last review particularly of any change in the care plan, whether decisions taken at the last review have been implemented and if not, why not
  - whether the responsible authority should seek any change in the child's legal status
  - whether there is a plan for permanence for the child
  - the arrangements for contact and whether there is any need for change in the arrangements
  - whether the placement continues to be the most appropriate for the child and whether any change in the child's accommodation arrangements is likely to be necessary or desirable before the next review
  - educational needs, progress and development and whether any change to the child's education or training arrangements are necessary or desirable,

having regard to the advice of any person who provides the child with education or training

- the child's leisure interests
- the report of the most recent assessment of the child's health and whether any changes to the arrangements for health care are necessary or desirable having regard to the advice of health care professionals
- whether the child's identity needs are being met, having regard to her/his religious persuasion, racial origin and cultural background
- whether the arrangements for the child to seek advice and assistance continue to be appropriate and whether s/he understands them
- whether any arrangements need to be made for the time when the child wil no longer be looked after
- the child's wishes and feelings and the views of the IRO about any aspect of the child's case and any changes made or proposed
- the frequency of the responsible authority's proposed visits to the child.

The role of the IRO [regs.36 & 45 CPPR 2010]

- The IRO must:
    - so far as reasonably practicable, attend the review meeting and if attending, chair it
    - speak to the child in private about the matters to be discussed at the review unless the child refuses or the IRO considers it inappropriate because of the child's age or understanding
    - ensure that, as far as reasonably practicable, the wishes and feelings of the child's parents and others with parental responsibility have been ascertained and taken into account
    - ensure that the persons responsible for implementing the decisions of the review are identified and
    - notify an officer of appropriate seniority in the LA of any failure to review

the child's case or implement the decisions taken as a consequence of the review.

- The IRO may adjourn the review meeting once for not more than 20 working days in order to obtain more information and any proposal put forward for consideration may not be implemented until the review has been completed.

- The IRO must ensure that, having regard to her/his age and understanding, the child has been informed by the responsible authority of the steps that s/he may take under the CA 1989, in particular:

  - the child's right to apply, with leave, for a Residence or Contact Order or discharge of any Care Order
  - the availability of the representation procedure established under section 26(3) CA 1989.

- If the child wishes to take legal proceedings, the IRO must establish whether an appropriate adult is willing and able to assist the child to obtain legal advice or bring proceedings on the child's behalf, and if not, to assist the child themselves.

- If the responsible authority:

  - have failed in any significant respect to prepare or review the child's care plan, or
  - have failed effectively to implement any decision taken as a consequence of a review, or
  - are in breach of their duties towards the child in any material respect and
  - have not addressed the failure within a reasonable time of the failure having been brought to the attention of a senior officer in the authority,

  the IRO must consider whether to refer the child's case to CAFCASS.

- If the responsible authority consults or informs the IRO about any matter concerning the child, the IRO must:

- ensure that the responsible authority have ascertained and given due consideration to the child's wishes and feelings and
- consider whether to request a review of the child's case.

Reviews of short-break placements with the same foster parent [reg.48 CPPR 2010]

- The CPPR 2010 apply, with modifications, to a series of short-term placements with the same carer or in the same accommodation if:
  - the child is not in the care of the responsible authority
  - no single placement is intended to last longer than seven days
  - at the end of each placement the child returns home to her/his parent or other person with parental responsibility
  - the short-breaks do not exceed 75 days in total in any 12-month period.
- The modifications that apply to short-break placements are:
  - regulations 5 (care plan) and 9 (placement plan) do not apply, but the care plan must set out the arrangements made to meet the child's needs with particular regard to:
    - the child's health and social development
    - promoting contact with parents or others while the child is placed
    - the child's leisure interests
    - promoting the child's educational acheivement
  - regulations 7 (health care), 13 (notification of placement) and 49(2)(b) (records – health care report) do not apply
  - regulation 28(2) (visits to the child) does not apply, but the child must be visited as set out on page 27 above
  - regulation 33 (reviews) does not apply, but the child's case must be

reviewed within three months of the start of the first placement and at intervals of no more than six months thereafter.

Independent visitors [s.23ZB & Sch.2 para.17 CA 1989 & reg.47 CPPR 2010]

- The LA must appoint an independent visitor (whose role is to visit, advise and befriend) when a child is looked after by an LA and:

  - contact with a parent or other person who has parental responsibility has been infrequent or
  - she/he has not visited, been visited or lived with any of these people during the last 12 months and
  - it would be in the best interests of the child.

  An independent visitor must be acceptable to a child and, if of sufficient understanding, she/he may refuse a proposed person. If the child has special needs, the visitor should have or be helped to develop relevant skills. An independent visitor is entitled to reclaim reasonable expenses from the LA.

- A person may only be regarded as independent of the responsible authority if she/he is:

  - not a member of the responsible authority or any of their committees or sub-committees
  - not employed in relation to any of the responsible authority's education or children's services functions
  - not a spouse, civil partner or other person living in the same household as a member or employee of the children's services of the responsible authority.

Complaints and representations [ss.26(3) to (9) & 59(4) CA 1989, Children Act 1989 Representations Procedure (England) Regulations 2006 (S.I. 1738), & reg.18 FSR 2011]

- Representations, including complaints about discharge of a local authority's functions under Part III CA 1989, and the provision by a voluntary organisation of accommodation to any child not looked after by a local authority, are provided for by sections 26(3)–(8) and 59(4) CA 1989 respectively.

- For issues not covered by the Children Act 1989 Representations Procedure (England) Regulations 2006, regulation 18 obliges the registered person of an independent fostering provider to establish a procedure for considering complaints made by or on behalf of children placed by the agency as well as foster parents approved by it [reg.18(1)].

- The procedure must in particular provide:
  - an opportunity for informal resolution of the complaint at an early stage
  - that no person subject to a complaint takes any part in its consideration other than if the registered person considers it appropriate, at the informal resolution stage only
  - for dealing with complaints about the registered person
  - for complaints to be made by a person acting on behalf of a child
  - for arrangements for the procedure to be made known to placed children, parents, and persons working for the purposes of the independent fostering agency [reg.18(2)].

- A copy of the procedure must be supplied on request to any of the above individuals and must include:
  - name, address and phone number of the Chief Inspector (OFSTED) and
  - details of procedure (if any) notified to the registered person by OFSTED for making complaints to it about the agency [reg.18(3)].

- The registered person must ensure that a record is made of any complaint, the action taken in response and the outcome of the investigation [reg.18(4)].
- The registered person must ensure that:
    - children are enabled to make a complaint or representation and
    - no child is subject to any reprisal for making a complaint or representation [reg.18(5)].
- The registered person must supply the Chief Inspector (OFSTED) with an annual summary of complaints made in the preceding 12 months and the action taken in response [reg.18(6)].

Advocacy services for children making a complaint against the local authority [The Children Act 1989 Representations Procedure (England) Regulations 2006]

- Local authorities have a duty to provide independent advocates to assist care leavers and children who intend to make representations under sections 24D and 26(3)(d) of the Children Act 1989.

Part II

The conduct of fostering agencies and local authority fostering services, and the assessment, approval and support of foster carers

The Fostering Services (England) Regulations 2011

General [regs.1-2 FSR 2011]

- The registered provider in relation to a fostering agency means a person who is registered under Part II of the CSA 2000 as the person carrying on the fostering agency [reg.2].

Statement of purpose and children's guide [regs.3 & 4]

- The fostering service provider must compile a 'statement of purpose' which includes:
    - the aims and objectives of the fostering service
    - a statement as to the services and facilities (including any parent and child arrangements) to be provided [reg.3(1)].
- The fostering service provider must provide a copy of the statement of purpose to the Chief Inspector (OFSTED) and make a copy of it available upon request, to:
    - any person working for the purpose of the fostering service
    - any foster parent or prospective foster parent of the service
    - any child placed with a foster parent by the fostering service and
    - the parent of any such child [reg.3(2)].
- The fostering service provider must also produce a 'children's guide' which includes:
    - a summary of the statement of purpose
    - a summary of the organisation's complaints procedure
    - address and telephone number of the Chief Inspector [reg.3(3)].
- The fostering service provider must provide copies of the children's guide to:
    - the Chief Inspector (OFSTED)

- each foster parent approved by the fostering service provider and
- (subject to age and understanding) each child placed by it [reg.3(4)].

- The fostering service provider must ensure that the fostering service is at all times conducted in a manner which is consistent with its statement of purpose, any conditions of registration and the FSR 2011 [reg.3(5) & (6)].

- The fostering service provider must:

  - keep under review and, where appropriate, revise the statement of purpose and children's guide
  - notify OFSTED within 28 days of any such revision and
  - ensure that each foster parent approved by it and (subject to age and understanding) each child placed by it, receives a copy of any revised children's guide [reg.4].

Local authority fostering services registered persons and management [regs.5-10 FSR 2011]

Fostering agency: Fitness of provider [reg.5]

- A person must not carry on a fostering agency unless she/he is fit to do so [reg.5(1)].

- A person is not fit to carry on a fostering agency either as an individual, a partner or an organisation, unless all specified requirements are satisfied [reg.5(2)].

- The requirements are that:

  - the individual (all individuals in the case of a partnership or, in the case of an organisation, a nominated 'responsible individual' who supervises the management of the agency) is of integrity and good character
  - she/he is physically and mentally fit to carry on a fostering agency

- full and satisfactory information is available about the person as detailed in Schedule 1 FSR 2011 [reg.5(2)].

- The information required in respect of persons seeking to carry on, manage or work for the purposes of a fostering service is in Schedule 1 as follows:

  - proof of identity including a recent photograph
  - either where the certificate is required for a purpose related to registration under Part II of the CSA 2000, or the position falls within regulation 5A of the Police Act 1997 (Criminal Records) Regulations 2002, an enhanced criminal record certificate issued under section 113B of the Police Act 1997, including suitability information relating to children, or in any other case, a standard criminal record certificate issued under section 113A of that Act
  - two written references, including a reference from the person's most recent employer, if any
  - where a person has previously worked in a position whose duties involved work with children or vulnerable adults, so far as reasonably practicable, verification of the reason why the employment or position ended
  - documentary evidence of any relevant qualification
  - a full employment history, together with a satisfactory written explanation of any gaps in employment.

- A person is not allowed to carry on a fostering agency if she/he is an un-discharged bankrupt or has made an arrangement with creditors in respect of which she/he has not been discharged [reg.5(3)].

Fostering agency: Appointment of manager [reg.6]

- The registered provider must appoint an individual to manage the fostering agency [reg.6(1)].

- Where the registered provider is an organisation, it must not appoint the person who is the responsible individual as the manager, or where the registered provider is a partnership, it must not appoint any of the partners as the manager [reg.6(2)].

- Where the registered provider appoints a person to manage the fostering agency, she/he must immediately give notice to OFSTED of the:
  - name of the person so appointed and
  - date on which the appointment is to take effect [reg.6(3)].

Fostering agency: Fitness of manager [reg.7]

- A person must not manage a fostering agency unless she/he is fit to do so [reg.7(1)].
- A person is not fit to manage a fostering agency unless:
  - she/he is of integrity and good character
  - having regard to agency's size, statement of purpose and numbers and needs of children placed by it, she/he is physically and mentally fit for the role
  - has the qualifications, skills and experience necessary for managing the fostering agency
  - full and satisfactory information is available in relation to her/him as detailed in Schedule 1 FSR [reg.7(2)].

Registered person: General requirements [reg.8]

- The registered provider and registered manager must, having regard to the agency's size, statement of purpose, and number and needs of children placed by it, and the need to safeguard and promote children placed, carry on/manage the fostering agency with sufficient care, competence and skill [reg.8(1)].
- From time to time, so as to ensure sufficient experience and skills necessary

for carrying on the agency, appropriate training must be completed (as is relevant) by:

- the registered provider (if she/he is an individual)
- the responsible individual (and the responsibility for ensuring this rests with the organisation which engages her/him)
- one member of any partnership [reg.8(2)].

- The registered manager must also undertake from time to time such training as is appropriate to ensure she/he has the experience and skills necessary for managing the fostering agency [reg.8(3)].

Notification of offences [reg.9]

- Where the registered person or the responsible individual is convicted of any criminal offence in England or Wales or elsewhere, she/he must without delay give notice to OFSTED of the:
  - date and place of the conviction
  - offence of which she/he was convicted
  - penalty imposed [reg.9(1)].

Local authority fostering service: Manager [reg.10]

- Each local authority must appoint one of its officers to manage its fostering services and notify OFSTED of the name of the appointee and the date on which the appointment is to take effect [reg.10(1)].

- The requirements in regulations 7, 8 and 9 (fitness of manager, general requirements of provider and manager, and notification of offences) are applicable to the manager of a local authority fostering service [reg.10(2)].

- The local authority must immediately notify OFSTED if the fostering services manager ceases to manage that service.

Conduct of fostering services (regs.11–18 FSR 2011]

Independent fostering agencies: Duty to secure welfare [reg.11]

- The registered person in respect of an independent fostering agency must ensure that:
  - the welfare of children placed or to be placed with foster parents is safeguarded and promoted at all times
  - before making any decisions affecting a child placed or to be placed, due consideration is given to the child's wishes and feelings in the light of her/his age and understanding, religious persuasion, racial origin and cultural and linguistic background [reg.11].

Also see pp.18–19.

NB. A voluntary organisation which places children with foster parents under section 59(1) CA 1989 has similar duties under section 61 CA 1989, as does a local authority under section 22 CA 1989.

Arrangements for the protection of children [reg.12]

- The fostering service provider must prepare and implement a written policy which:
  - is intended to safeguard children placed with foster parents from abuse or neglect, and
  - sets out the procedure to be followed in the event of any allegation of abuse or neglect [reg.12(1)].

Also see pp.19–20.

Behaviour management and children missing from foster parent's home [reg.13]

- The fostering service provider must prepare and implement a written policy on acceptable measures of control, restraint and discipline of children placed with foster parents [reg.13(1)].

- The fostering service provider must prepare and implement a written procedure to be followed if a child is missing from a foster parent's home without permission [reg.13(3)].

Also see pp.20–21.

Duty to promote contact [reg.14]

- The fostering service provider must (subject to the child's care plan and any court order about contact) promote contact between a child placed with a foster parent and the child's parents, relatives and friends unless such contact is not reasonably practicable or consistent with the child's welfare.

- Also see p.25.

Health of children placed with foster parents [reg.15]

- The service provider must promote the health and development of children placed with foster parents.

Also see pp.21–23.

Education, employment and leisure activities [reg.16]

- The FSP must promote the educational attainment of children who are placed with foster parents [reg.16(1)].

- The FSP must

  - implement a procedure for monitoring the educational achievement, progress and school attendance of children placed with foster parents

  - promote the regular school attendance and participation in school activities of children of compulsory school age placed with foster parents

- provide foster parents with information and assistance, including equipment, to meet the educational needs of children placed with them [reg.16(2)]
- ensure any education it provides for any child placed with foster parents who is of compulsory school age but not attending, is efficient and suitable to the child's age, ability, aptitude, and any special educational needs she/he may have [reg.16(3)].

- The fostering service provider must ensure that foster parents promote the leisure interests of children placed with them [reg.16(4)].
- Where any child placed with foster parents is above compulsory school age, the fostering service provider must assist with making of and giving effect to arrangements for the child's education, training and employment [reg.16(5)].

Also see pp.23–24.

Support, training and information for foster parents [reg.17]

- The fostering service provider must provide foster parents with such training, advice, information and support (including support in out-of-office hours) as appears necessary in the interests of children placed with them [reg.17(1)].

Also see pp.24–25.

Independent fostering agencies: Representations and complaints [reg.18]

- Representations, including complaints about discharge of a local authority's functions under Part III CA 1989, and the provision by a voluntary organisation of accommodation to any child not looked after by a local authority, are provided for by sections 26(3)–(8) and 59(4) CA 1989 respectively.

- For issues not covered by the Children Act 1989 Representations Procedure (England) Regulations 2006, regulation 18 obliges the registered person of an IFA to establish a procedure for considering complaints made by or on behalf of children placed by the agency as well as foster parents approved by it [reg.18(1)].

Also see pp.34–35.

Staffing and employment [regs.19–21 FSR 2011]

Staffing of fostering service [reg.19]

- The fostering service provider must ensure that there is at all times a sufficient number of suitably qualified, competent and experienced persons working for the purposes of the fostering service having regard to the:
  - size of the service, its statement of purpose and the number and needs of the children placed by it
  - need to safeguard and promote the health and welfare of children placed with foster parents.

Fitness of workers [reg.20]

- The fostering service provider must not, unless the person in question is fit to work for the purposes of the fostering service:
  - employ a person to work for the purposes of the fostering service
  - allow a person who is employed by someone other than the registered person to work in the service in a position in which she/he may in the course of her/his duties have regular contact with children placed by the service [reg.20(1)].
- A person is not 'fit' to work for the purposes of a fostering service unless:
  - she/he is of integrity and good character

- has the qualifications, skills and experience necessary for the work she/he is to perform
- is physically and mentally fit for the purposes of the work to be performed and
- full and satisfactory information is available about her/him as per Schedule 1 FSR 2011, which includes:
  - proof of identity, including a photograph
  - the appropriate CRB certificate
  - two written references, one from the person's most recent employer
  - the reason why any previous employment with children or vulnerable adults ended
  - documentary evidence of qualifications
  - a full employment history, covering any gaps in employment.

■ The service provider must also take reasonable steps to ensure that any person working for the FSP who is not employed by the FSP and does not have regular contact with children placed are appropriately supervised while working for the FSP.

Employment of staff [reg.21]

■ The fostering service provider must:

- ensure all permanent appointments are subject to satisfactory completion of a probation period
- provide all employees with a job description [reg.21(1)].

■ The fostering service provider must operate a disciplinary procedure which, in particular:

- provides for the suspension of an employee where necessary in the interests of the safety or welfare of children placed with foster parents

- provides that failure on the part of an employee to report to an appropriate person, an incident of abuse, or suspected abuse, of a child placed with foster parents is a ground on which disciplinary proceedings may be instituted [reg.21(2)].

- An 'appropriate person' for the above purpose is:

  - in all cases, the registered person/manager of local authority fostering service, an officer of OFSTED, an officer of the responsible, or area, authority if applicable or a police officer or an officer of the NSPCC
  - for an employee of an IFA, an officer of the responsible authority and
  - for an employee of a fostering agency, an officer of the local authority in whose area the agency is situated [reg.21(3)].

- The fostering service provider must ensure that all persons employed by them:

  - receive appropriate training, supervision and appraisal and
  - are enabled from time to time to obtain further qualifications appropriate to the work they perform [reg.21(4)].

Records [reg.22 FSR 2011]

Records with respect to fostering services [reg.22 & Sch. 2]

- The fostering service provider must maintain and keep up to date (as per Schedule 2) a register which records, with respect to each child placed with foster parents:

  - date of the placement
  - name and address of the foster parent
  - date on which the child ceased to be placed there
  - address prior to the placement
  - address on leaving the placement

- responsible authority (if it is not the FSP)
- the statutory provision under which the child was placed with foster parents.

- The fostering service provider must also maintain and keep up to date a record showing in respect of each person working for the fostering service provider:

  - her/his full name
  - her/his sex
  - date of birth and
  - home address
  - qualifications relevant to and experience of work involving children
  - whether employed by the provider under a contract of service or a contract for services, or employed by someone other than the fostering service provider
  - whether she/he works full- or part-time and if part-time, the average number of hours worked per week.

- The fostering service provider must also maintain a record of all accidents occurring to children whilst placed with foster parents.

- All the above records must be retained for a period of 15 years from the date of last entry [reg.22(2)].

Fostering panels [regs.23–25 FSR 2011]

The constitution of fostering panels [reg.23]

- The FSP must maintain a 'central list' of people who are considered suitable to be members of the fostering panel, including at least one social worker who has at least three years relevant post-qualification experience [reg.23(1)].

- a person included in the central list may ask to be removed from the list by giving one month's written notice [reg.23(2)]
- the FSP may remove the name of any person from the list by giving one month's written notice, if they are of the opinion that the person is unsuitable or unable to remain on the list [reg 23(3)]
- the FSP must constitute one or more fostering panels from the persons on the central list [reg.23(4)]
- two or more FSPs may constitute a joint fostering panel, appointing members by agreement between the FSPs [reg.23(5)].

Chair of panel [reg.23(4)]

- The FSP must appoint a person from the central list to chair the panel:
  - after 1 October 2011 the Chair of the panel must be an independent person
  - a person is not independent if they are approved by the FSP as a foster parent, an elected member of an LA of employed by the LA for the purposes of the fostering service or child protection or placement (for an LA FSP), or employed by or a trustee of the FSP (for an IFA).

Vice-chair of panel

- The FSP must appoint one or two persons from the central list who will act as chair if the appointed individual is absent or the office is vacant [reg.23(4)]. It is recommended, although not required, that the vice-chair is also independent of the FSP.

Panel members

- Any panel member may resign office at any time by giving a month's written notice to the FSP [reg.23(8)].
- Where an FSP is of the opinion that any panel member is unsuitable or unable to continue as a panel member, it may terminate her/his appointment at any time by giving written notice [reg.23(9)].

Meetings of fostering panel [reg.24]

- No business may be conducted by a panel unless at least:

  - the Chair or one of the vice-chairs;
  - one member who is a social worker (who may or may not be employed by the FSP) with at least three years' relevant post-qualifying experience and
  - three other members (or four if a joint panel)

  meet as a panel. At least one member of the panel present, who may be the Chair or vice-chair, must be independent of the FSP [reg.24(1)].

Panel minutes and recommendations and reasons [reg.24]

- A panel must make a written record of its proceedings and the reasons for its recommendation [reg.24(2)].

Functions of fostering panel [reg.25]

- The functions of the fostering panel are:

  - to consider each application for approval and to recommend (to the service provider) whether or not a person is suitable to be a foster parent
  - where it recommends approval, to recommend any terms on which the approval is to be given
  - to recommend whether a person remains suitable to be a foster parent, and whether the terms of her/his approval remain appropriate, on the first annual review and on any other occasion when it is invited to do so (see below)
  - to consider further any written representations challenging a determination by the service provider not to approve an individual (see below) which are referred to it by the service provider
  - to consider further any written representations challenging a determination by the service provider to terminate, or revise the terms of,

the approval of an individual (see below) which are referred to it by the service provider [reg.25(1)].

- The fostering panel must also:
  - advise on the procedures under which 'regulation 28' reviews of foster parents are carried out by the fostering service provider and periodically monitor their effectiveness
  - oversee the conduct of assessments carried out by the fostering provider and
  - give advice and make recommendations on such matters or cases as the fostering service provider may refer to it [reg.25(4)].

Assessment and approval [regs.26, 27 & 28 FSR 2011 & Sch. 3]

Assessment of prospective foster parents [reg.26 & Sch. 3]

- The FSP may carry out an assessment of any person who applies and whom it considers may be suitable to become a foster parent, in accordance with regulation 26 [reg.26(1)].
- If the FSP considers that a person may be suitable to act as a foster parent, it must:
  - obtain the information specified in Schedule 3 relating to the prospective foster parent and other members of her/his household and family and any other information it considers relevant
  - interview at least two persons nominated by the prospective foster parent to provide personal references for her/him, and prepare written reports of the interviews
  - (unless the service provider is a local authority and the applicant lives within that authority) consult with and take into account the views of the local authority where the prospective foster parent lives

- inspect the records of another FSP, where the prospective foster parent has been approved and his/her approval terminated by the other FSP, if the prospective foster carer consents [reg.26(2)].

■ Having regard to the information obtained, the FSP must:

- consider whether the applicant is suitable to be a foster parent and whether the household is suitable for any child
- prepare a written report on her/him which includes:
  - the information required by Schedule 3 and any other information the FSP considers relevant
  - the FSP's assessment of her/his suitability to be a foster parent and
  - the FSP's proposals about any terms of approval [reg.26(4)]
- refer the report to the fostering panel and notify the prospective foster parent accordingly [reg.26(3)].

Schedule 3

■ Schedule 3 specifies the following information which is required with respect to the prospective foster parent:

- full name, address and date of birth
- details of health (supported by a medical report), personality, marital status and details of current and any previous marriage, civil partnership or similar relationship
- particulars of other adults in her/his household
- particulars of the children in her/his family, whether or not members of the household and any other children in the household
- particulars of her/his accommodation
- her/his religious persuasion and capacity to care for a child from any particular religious persuasion

- racial origin, cultural and linguistic background and capacity to care for a child from any particular such background
- past and present employment or occupation, standard of living and leisure activities and interests
- previous experience (if any) of caring for her/his own and other children
- skills, competence and potential relevant to her/his capacity to care effectively for a child placed with her/him
- the outcome of any request or application made by her/him or any other household member to foster or adopt, register as an early years or later years provider, including particulars of any previous approval or refusal of approval relating to her/him or to any other household member
- names and addresses of two persons who will provide personal references for the prospective foster parent.

Criminal convictions and cautions

- Schedule 3 also requires, in relation to the prospective foster parent and any other adult member of the household, an enhanced criminal record certificate issued under section 113B Police Act 1997 (PA 1997) (to include suitability information relating to children).

Prohibition on approval for specified offences or cautions [reg.26(5) & (7)]

- A person must not be regarded as suitable to be a foster parent if she/he or any member of the household aged 18 or over:
  - has been convicted of a specified offence committed at the age of 18 or over or
  - has been cautioned by police in respect of any such offence [reg.26(5)].
- The FSP may, however, consider such a person as suitable to be a foster parent for a particular child or children if the FSP is satisfied that the welfare of that child or those children requires it and the person or a member of

her/his household is a relative of the child or the person is already acting as a foster parent for the child [reg.26(8)].

- 'Specified offence' is defined in regulation 26(6) Fostering Services Regulations 2011.

Approval of foster parents [reg.27]

- A foster parent may only be approved by one FSP at any one time.
- An FSP must not approve a person who has been approved as a foster parent by another FSP and whose approval has not been terminated [reg.27(1)].
- An FSP must not approve a person as a foster parent unless:
  - it has completed its assessment of her/his suitability and
  - its fostering panel has considered the application [reg.27(2)] (see section on Fostering Panels, pp.50–53).
- An FSP must, in deciding whether to approve a person as a foster parent and as to terms of approval, take into account the recommendation of its fostering panel [reg.27(3)].
- No member of its fostering panel may take part in any such decision made by an FSP [reg.27(4)].
- If an FSP decides to approve a person as a foster parent, it must:
  - give her/him written notice specifying terms of approval e.g. in respect of a named child/ren, number and age range of children, or of placements of any particular kind, or in any particular circumstances
  - enter into a written agreement covering the matters specified in Schedule 5 below (the foster care agreement) [reg.27(5)].

Foster care agreements [Sch. 5]

- Schedule 5 specifies the matters and obligations in foster care agreements as follows:

  - terms of the foster parent's approval
  - the support and training to be given to the foster parent
  - procedure for review of approval
  - procedures in connection with placement of children and matters to be included in any placement plan
  - arrangements for meeting any legal liabilities of the foster parent arising by reason of a placement
  - procedure available to foster parents for making representations or complaints.

- the foster parent's obligations are:

  - to care for any child as if she/he were a member of the family and to promote her/his welfare having regard to the long- and short-term plans for her/him
  - to give written notice to the service provider, with full particulars of any intended change of address or household composition, any other change in personal circumstance and any other event affecting capacity to care for any child placed or suitability of household, and any request or application to adopt or for registration as an early or later years provider
  - not to administer corporal punishment to any child placed with her/him
  - to ensure any information relating to a placed child, to the child's family or any other person, given in confidence in connection with the placement, is kept confidential and not disclosed to anyone without consent of the FSP
  - to comply with the terms of any placement plan
  - to comply with policies and procedures of the FSP issued under regulations 12 and 13 (see above)

- to co-operate as reasonably required with OFSTED and, in particular, to allow a person authorised by OFSTED to interview her/him and visit her/his home at any reasonable time
- to keep the FSP informed about the child's progress and notify it immediately of any significant events affecting the child.

Applicants not suitable for approval as foster carers [reg.27(6) & (9)]

- If an FSP considers that a person is not suitable to be a foster parent it must:
  - give her/him written notice that it proposes not to approve her/him (this is a 'Qualifying Determination'), together with its reasons and a copy of the fostering panel's recommendations
  - advise her/him that within 28 days of the date of the qualifying determination she/he may
    - submit written representations to the FSP or
    - apply to the IRM for a review of the Qualifying Determination [reg.27(6)].
- If the FSP does not receive any representations within 28 days and no application is made to the IRM, it may proceed to make its decision [reg.27(8)].
- If the FSP receives any written representations within 28 days, it must:
  - refer the case to the fostering panel for further consideration and
  - make its decision, taking into account any fresh recommendations made by the fostering panel [reg.27(9)].
- If the prospective foster carer applies to the IRM within 28 days, the FSP must make its decision, taking into account the recommendation of the fostering panel and of the independent review panel.

- As soon as practicable after making the decision with respect to approval, the FSP must notify the prospective foster parent in writing and:
  - if the decision is to approve the person, give notice of any terms of approval and sign a foster care agreement
  - if the decision is not to approve the person, provide written reasons for its decision [reg.27(11)].

Reviews of approval as foster carers [reg.28]

- The service provider must review approval of each foster parent in accordance with regulation 28 [reg.28(1)].
- A review must take place not more than a year after approval, and thereafter whenever the service provider considers it necessary, but at intervals of not more than a year [reg.28(2)].
- When undertaking a review, the fostering service provider must:
  - make such enquiries and obtain such information as it considers necessary to review whether the person continues to be suitable to be a foster parent and her/his household continues to be suitable
  - seek and take into account the views of the foster parent and (subject to age and understanding) any child placed with the foster parent and any responsible authority which has within the preceding year placed a child with the foster parent [reg.28(3)].
- At the conclusion of the review the service provider must prepare a written report, setting out whether:
  - the person continues to be suitable to be a foster parent and her/his household continues to be suitable
  - the terms of her/his approval continue to be appropriate [reg.28(4)].

First reviews referred to fostering panel

- The FSP must, for the first review and may, on any subsequent review, refer its report to the fostering panel for consideration [reg.28(5)].

Termination of approval as foster carers or variation in terms of approval [reg.28]

- If the FSP decides, taking into account any recommendation made by the fostering panel, that the foster parent and household continue to be suitable and terms of approval continue to be appropriate, it must give written notice to the foster parent of its decision [reg.28(6)].

- If, taking into account any recommendation made by the panel, the service provider is no longer satisfied the foster parent and her/his household continue to be suitable, or that terms of approval are appropriate, it must:

  - notify the foster parent in writing (a "qualifying determination") that it proposes to terminate, or revise terms of her/his approval as the case may be, together with its reasons and a copy of the panel recommendations, and
  - advise her/him that she/he may either submit any written representations within 28 days of the date of the notice [reg.28(7)] or
  - apply to the IRM for a review of the qualifying determination [reg.28(7)].

- If the service provider does not receive any representations and the foster parent does not apply to the IRM within 28 days it may proceed to make its decision [reg.28(9)]. There is no provision for shortening this period, even if the foster parent has consented to a variation in their terms of approval.

- If the service provider does receive any written representations within 28 days, it must:

  - refer the case to the fostering panel for its consideration and
  - make its decision, taking into account any recommendation made by the panel [reg.28(10)].

- If the foster parent applies to the IRM within 28 days, the FSP must make its decision, taking into account the recommendation of the fostering panel and of the independent review panel [reg.28(11)].

- As soon as practicable after making its final decision as described above, the service provider must write to the foster parent stating:

  - the foster parent and her/his household continue to be suitable, and the terms of the approval continue to be appropriate or
  - her/his approval is terminated from a specified date, and the reasons for the termination or
  - the revised terms of the approval and the reasons for the revision [reg.28(12)].

- A foster parent may give notice in writing to the FSP at any time that she/he no longer wishes to be a foster parent, whereupon her/his approval is terminated with effect from 28 days from the date on which the notice is received by the FSP [reg.28(13)].

- A copy of any notice given under this regulation shall be sent to the responsible authority for any child placed with the foster parent (unless the responsible authority is also the FSP) and to the area authority [reg.28(14)].

- A copy of the notice must also be sent to the Secretary of State in any case where the IRM has made a recommendation [reg.28(15)]

Information to be sent to the independent review panel [reg.29 FSR 2011]

- Where a person has applied for an independent review of a qualifying determination the Secretary of State will send notification to the FSP. Within ten working days of receipt of the notification the FSP must send to the IRM:

- a copy of any report prepared and any other documents referred to the fostering panel
- any other relevant information obtained after the report was prepared
- a copy of the notice of the qualifying determination and of any other documents sent to the prospective foster carer or foster carer [reg.29(2)].

Case records [regs.30–32 FSR 2011]

Case records relating to foster parents and others [reg.30]

- An FSP must maintain a case record for each foster parent approved by it which must include the following documents:
    - notice of approval given under regulation 27(5)(a)
    - foster care agreement
    - any report of a review of approval prepared under regulation 28(4)
    - any notice given under regulation 28(12)
    - any agreement entered into in accordance with regulation 38(1)(a)
    - the report prepared under regulation 26(3)(b) and any other reports submitted to the fostering panel and
    - any recommendations made by the fostering panel.
- The case record must also include the following information:
    - a record of each placement with the foster parent, including name, age and sex of each child placed, dates on which each placement began and terminated and the circumstances of the termination
    - the information obtained by the FSP in relation to the assessment and approval of the foster parent and in relation to any review or termination of the approval.

- A local authority must maintain a case record for each person given temporary approval as a foster carer as a person connected with a child under regulation 24 CPPR 2010 which must include:

  - a record of the placement, including name, age and sex of each child placed, dates on which each placement began and if the placement has been terminated, the date and the circumstances of the termination
  - the information obtained in relation to the enquiries carried out under regulation 24(2) of the CPPR 2010.

Record of persons not approved as foster parents [reg.30(5)]

- The FSP shall compile a record for each person whom it does not approve as a foster parent, or who withdraws her/his application prior to approval, which must include in relation to her/him:

  - the information obtained in connection with the assessment
  - any report submitted to the fostering panel and any recommendation made by the fostering panel and
  - any notification given under regulation 27.

Register of foster parents [reg.31]

- The FSP must enter in a register kept for the purpose the:

  - name, address, date of birth and sex of each foster parent and connected person with temporary approval as a foster parent under regulation 24 CPPR 2010
  - date of her/his approval and of each review of her/his approval and
  - current terms of her/his approval.

Retention and confidentiality of records [reg.32]

- Records compiled in relation to a foster parent under regulation 30(1), and any entry relating to her/him in the register maintained under regulation

31(1) must be retained for at least 10 years from the date on which approval is terminated [reg.32(1)].

- Records compiled by a local authority under regulation 30(4) in relation to a person with whom a child is placed under regulation 24 CPPR 2010, and any entry relating to such a person in the register maintained under regulation 31(1), must be retained for at least 10 years from the date on which the placement is terminated [reg.32(2)].

- Records compiled under regulation 30(5) must be retained for at least three years from refusal or withdrawal of the application to become a foster parent [reg.32(3)].

- These requirements may be complied with by retaining the original written records or copies, or by keeping all or part of the information contained in them in another accessible form e.g. computer record [reg.32(4)].

- Any records or register maintained in accordance with regulation 22, 30 or 31 must be kept securely and may not be disclosed to any person except in accordance with any:

  - provision of, or made under, or by virtue of, a statute under which access to such records is authorised or any
  - court order authorising access to such records
  - an FSP must make their records in relation to a foster parent available to another FSP within one month of a request under regulation 26(2)(d).

Placements [CPPR 2010]

See also pp10–18.

Making of placements [reg.22 CPPR 2010]

- Except in the case of an emergency placement under regulation 23, a responsible authority may only place a child with a foster parent if:

- the foster parent is approved by the responsible authority proposing to make the placement or provided the conditions specified in regulation 22(3) (immediately below) are satisfied, by another FSP
- the terms of approval are consistent with the proposed placement [reg.22(2)(b)] and she/he has entered into a foster care agreement [reg.22(2)(c)].

- The conditions referred to in regulation 22(2)(a)(i) are:
  - that the service provider, by whom the foster parent is approved, consents to the placement
  - that any other responsible authority, which already has a child placed with the foster parent, consents to the placement.
- Before making a placement, the responsible authority must prepare a placement plan for the child which covers the matters specified in Schedule 2 [reg.9(1)].
- Schedule 2 specifies the following matters and obligations to be covered in the child's placement plan when the child is to be placed with foster carers.
  - how the child will be cared for and her/his welfare will be safeguarded and promoted
  - any arrangements made for contact between the child and her/his parents and any other appropriate person
  - any reasons why contact with any person would not be reasonably practicable or inconsistent with the child's welfare
  - if the child is not in the care of the responsible authority, details of any order made under section 8 (residence, contact or specific issues)
  - if the child is in the care of the responsible authority, details of any contact order made under section 34

- the arrangements for notifying any changes in the arrangements for contact
- the arrangements made for the child's health (including physical, emotional and mental health) and dental care including –
  - the name and address of the child's registered medical and dental practitioners or those with whom the child is to be registered after placement
  - any arrangements for the giving or withholding of consent to medical or dental examination or treatment
- the arrangements made for education and training including –
  - the name and address of any school at which the child is registered
  - the name of the designated teacher at the school (if applicable)
  - the name and address of any other source of education or training that the child receives
  - where the child has a statement of special educational needs, details of the local authority that maintains the statement
- the arrangements made for a local authority to visit the child in accordance with Part 5, and the arrangements made for advice, support and assistance to be available to the child between visits in accordance with regulation 31
- if an independent visitor is appointed, the arrangements made for them to visit the child
- the circumstances in which the placement may be terminated and the child removed from the foster carer's care in accordance with regulation 14
- the name and contact details of –
  - the IRO
  - the child's independent visitor (if one is appointed)
  - the representative of the responsible authority, and

- if the child is an eligible child (CA 1989 Sch.2 para.19(b)), the personal adviser appointed for her

- the type of accommodation to be provided and the address
- the child's personal history, religious persuasion, cultural and linguistic background, and racial origin
- where the child is not in the care of the responsible authority –
  - the respective responsibilities of the responsible authority and the child's parents, or any person who has parental responsibility
  - any delegation of responsibility there has been by the child's parents, or any person who has parental responsibility
  - the expected duration of the arrangements and the steps which should be taken to bring the arrangements to an end, including arrangements for the child to return home, and
  - the fact that the child is over 16 and agrees to being accommodated under section 20
- the circumstances in which the foster carer will need to obtain the responsible authority's approval for the child to take part in school trips or to stay overnight away from the placement
- the responsible authority's arrangements for the financial support of the child during the placement
- the obligation on the foster carer to comply with the terms of the foster care agreement made under regulation 27(5)(b) FSR 2011.

Supervision of placements [reg.28 CPPR 2010]

- The responsible authority must supervise the child's welfare by visiting the child where she/he is living:

  - within one week of placement
  - at least every six weeks for the first year of placement, and

i. at least every three months if the placement is intended to continue until the child is 18 and

ii. in any other case, at least every six weeks [reg.28(2)]

- where the child is placed with a connected person temporarily approved as a foster carer, every week until the first review, then at least every four weeks [reg.28(4)].

The responsible authority must also ensure that the child is visited:

- whenever reasonably requested to do so by the child or her carer [reg.28(7)].

- On each visit the person responsible for carrying out the visit must speak to the child alone unless:
  - she/he, being of sufficient age and understanding to do so, refuses or
  - it is inappropriate to do so having regard to the child's age and understanding or they are unable to do so.

Termination of placements [reg.14 CPPR 2010]

- A responsible authority may only terminate a placement following a review of the child's case unless the child or others are at risk of serious harm or the foster carer ceases to be approved to care for the child [reg.14(1)].

- Before terminating a placement the responsible authority must make other arrangements for the child's accommodation, inform the IRO and notify their intention to terminate the placement to all persons who had notification of the placement, the foster carer and the area authority [reg.14(2)].

- If it is not possible to notify a person before the placement is terminated, written notice must be given within ten days of the placement being terminated [reg.14(4)].

Short-term placements [reg.48 CPPR 2010]

- Where a responsible authority has arranged to place a child in a series of short-term placements with the same foster parent and the arrangement is such that:

  - no single placement is intended to last for more than 17 days and
  - after each placement the child returns home and the total duration of the placements is not to exceed 75 days in any period of 12 months [reg.48(2)].

  The CPPR 2010 apply with the following modifications:

  - regulation 28(2) (visiting) does not apply, but instead the responsible authority must ensure that the child is visited when she/he is in fact placed, at regular intervals to be agreed with the IRO and the child's parents and recorded in the care plan before the start of the first placement, and in any event –
  - the first visit must take place within three months of the start of the first placement, or as soon as practicable thereafter, and
  - subsequent visits must take place at intervals of not more than six months, for as long as the short breaks continue
  - regulation 33 (case reviews) does not apply, but instead –
  - the responsible authority must first review the child's case within three months of the start of the first placement, and
  - the second and subsequent reviews must be carried out at intervals of not more than six months.

Fostering agencies - Miscellaneous [regs.33-41 FSR 2011]

Review of quality of care [reg.35]

- The registered person must maintain a system for:

- monitoring the matters set out in Schedule 6 at appropriate intervals and
- improving the quality of foster care provided by the fostering agency [reg.35(1)].

■ The matters in Schedule 6 to be monitored by the registered person are:

- compliance in relation to each child placed with foster parents, with the child's care plan
- all accidents, injuries and illnesses of children placed with foster parents
- complaints in relation to children placed with foster parents and their outcomes
- any allegations or suspicions of abuse or neglect in respect of children placed with foster parents and the outcome of any investigation
- recruitment records and conduct of required checks of new workers
- notification of events listed in Schedule 7 (see regulation 36 below)
- any unauthorised absence from the foster home of a child accommodated there
- use of any measure of control, restraint or discipline in respect of children accommodated in a foster home
- medication, medical treatment and first aid administered to any child placed with foster parents
- where applicable, the standard of any education provided by the fostering service
- records of assessments
- records of fostering panel meetings
- records of appraisal of employees
- minutes of staff meetings.

■ The registered person must supply to OFSTED a report in respect of any review conducted by her/him for the purposes of regulation 35(1) and make a copy of the report available upon request to any local authority [reg.35(2)].

- The system referred to in regulation 35(1) must provide for consultation with foster parents, children placed with foster parents, and their responsible authority (unless, in the case of a fostering agency which is a voluntary organisation, it is also the responsible authority).

Notifiable events [reg.36]

- If, in relation to a fostering agency, any of the events listed in column 1 of the table in Schedule 7 (summarised on the next page) takes place, the registered person must without delay notify the persons indicated in respect of the event in column 2 of the table [reg.36(1)].

- Any notification made in accordance with this regulation which is given orally must be confirmed in writing [reg.36(2)].

Financial position [reg.37]

- The registered provider must carry on the agency in such manner as is likely to ensure it will be financially viable for the purpose of achieving the aims and objectives set out in its statement of purpose [reg.37(1)].

- The registered provider must:

  - ensure that adequate accounts are maintained and kept up to date in respect of the fostering agency
  - supply a copy of the accounts, on request, to OFSTED [reg.37(2)].

- The registered provider must provide OFSTED with such information as it may require for the purpose of considering the financial viability of the fostering agency, including:

  - the annual accounts of the fostering agency, certified by an accountant

Event	To be notified to:					
	Chief Inspector	Responsible authority	Secretary of State	Area authority	Police	Primary Care Trust
Death of a child	x	x	x	x		x
Information provided to ISA under SVGA 2006* re individual	x	x				
Serious illness/accident of a child	x	x				
Serious infectious disease	x	x				x
Allegation of serious offence by child		x			x	
Suspected involvement of a child in prostitution	x	x		x	x	
Serious incident involving calling the police to the foster parent's home	x	x				
A child missing from the placement		x				
Any serious complaint about any foster parent	x	x				
Instigation and outcome of child protection enquiry	x	x		x		

* Safeguarding Vulnerable Groups Act 2006

- a reference from a bank expressing an opinion as to the registered provider's financial standing
- information as to the financing and financial resources of the fostering agency
- where the registered provider is a company, information as to any of its associated companies
- a certificate of insurance for the registered provider in respect of liability which may be incurred by her/him in relation to the fostering agency in respect of death, injury, public liability, damage or other loss [reg.37(3)].

- In this regulation, one company is associated with another if one of them has control of the other, or both are under the control of the same person or company [reg.37 (4)].

Notice of absence of registered manager of fostering agency [reg.38]

- Where the registered manager proposes to be absent from the agency for a continuous period of 28 days or more, the registered person must give notice in writing to OFSTED of the proposed absence [reg.38(1)].

- Except in an emergency, the notice referred to above must be given no later than one month before the proposed absence is to start, or within such shorter period as may be agreed with OFSTED, and the notice must specify:

  - length or expected length of proposed absence
  - reason for the proposed absence
  - arrangements which have been made for the running of the agency during that absence
  - name, address and qualifications of person responsible for the agency during the absence
  - arrangements that have been made or are proposed to be made for appointing another person to manage the agency during the absence,

including the proposed date by which the appointment is to start [reg.38(2)].

- Where absence arises as a result of an emergency, the registered person must give notice of it within one week of its occurrence, specifying the matters mentioned in regulation 38(2)(a) to (e) (summarised above) [reg.38(3)].

- Where the registered manager has been absent from the fostering agency for a continuous period of 28 days or more, and OFSTED has not been given notice of the absence, the registered person must without delay give notice in writing to OFSTED specifying the regulation 38(2) matters described in bullet points above [reg.38(4)].

- The registered person must notify OFSTED of the return to duty of the registered manager not later than seven days after the date of her/his return [reg.38(5)].

Notice of changes to management or operation of a fostering agency [reg.39]

- The registered person must give notice in writing to OFSTED without delay if any of the following events takes place or is proposed to take place:

  - a person other than the registered person carries on or manages the fostering agency
  - a person ceases to carry on or manage the fostering agency
  - where the registered provider is an individual, she/he changes her/his name
  - where the registered provider is a partnership, there is any change in the membership of the partnership
  - where the registered provider is an organisation, its name or address is changed, there is any change of director, manager, secretary or other

similar officer of the organisation, there is to be any change in the identity of the responsible individual

- where the registered provider is an individual, a trustee in bankruptcy is appointed or she/he makes any composition or arrangement with her/his creditors or
- where the registered provider is a company, or a partnership, a receiver, manager, liquidator or provisional liquidator is appointed in respect of the registered provider [reg.39(1)].

- The registered provider must notify OFSTED in writing and without delay of the death of the registered manager [reg.39(2)].

Appointment of liquidators, etc [reg.40]

- The receiver or manager of the property of a company or partnership which is a registered provider of a fostering agency, a liquidator or provisional liquidator of a company which is the registered provider of a fostering agency or the trustee in bankruptcy of a registered provider of a fostering agency must:
  - immediately notify OFSTED of her/his appointment indicating the reasons for it
  - appoint a manager to take full-time day-to-day charge of the fostering agency in any case where there is no registered manager and
  - not more than 28 days after appointment, notify OFSTED of her/his intentions regarding the future operation of the fostering agency [reg.40(1) and (2)].

Offences [s.22A Care Standards Act 2000]

- Where the Chief Inspector considers that the registered person is failing or has failed to comply with any of the provisions of regulations, it may serve a compliance notice on the registered person specifying:

- how it considers that the registered person has failed or is failing to comply with requirements of any of the regulations
- what action, in the opinion of the Chief Inspector, the registered person should take so as to comply with any of those regulations, or prevent a recurrence of a failure to comply
- the period within which the registered person should take action.

- Failing to take the steps specified in a compliance notice within the specified period is an offence [s.22A(4) CSA 2000]

Compliance with regulations [reg.41]

- Where there is more than one registered person in respect of an agency, anything required under these regulations to be done by the registered person is, if done by one of the registered persons, not required to be done by any of the other registered persons.

Miscellaneous [regs.42–45 FSR 2011]

Amendment and revocation of regulations [regs.43 & 44] and transitional provisions [reg.45]

- Regulation 43 amends the CPPR 2010 by substituting the words 'the Fostering Services (England) Regulations 2011' for 'the 2002 Regulations' and amending the regulation numbers as appropriate.

- Regulation 44 revokes the Fostering Services Regulations 2002.

- Regulation 45 allows a fostering panel established under the 2002 regulations to continue to carry out the functions of a panel under the 2011 regulations in respect of any case referred before 1 April 2011.

Fostering allowances [s.22C(10) CA 1989

- Local authorities are responsible for maintaining children they are looking after. The FSP will determine the amount of the allowance paid to its foster carers. The amounts payable, and the basis upon which it is calculated, varies between FSPs, including local authorities.

- Most IFAs and some local authorities pay allowances that include a reward element.

- The Fostering Network publishes recommended minimum weekly allowances for fostering in the UK, which vary according to the age of the child. These are designed to cover the cost of looking after a fostered child, and do not include any form of reward for the carer. Updated allowances are available on the Fostering Network's website at: www.fostering.net/resources/statistics/recommended-minimum-allowances.

- The Department for Education also publishes recommended minimum fostering rates on their website at: http://media.education.gov.uk/assets/files/pdf/n/national%20minimum%20allowance%20rates%20for%20fostering%20to%202012%2013.pdf.

Income tax and fostering allowances [Finance Act 2003]

- Foster carers have specific tax arrangements applied to their fostering income. Each fostering household is entitled to receive a 'qualifying amount' on which no income tax will be due.

- The qualifying amount consists of two elements:

- 1. The first £10,000 per year of their fostering income.

- 2. An additional amount for every week (or part week) that a child is fostered with them. For every week that a child aged 11 or older is in placement, the foster carer's qualifying amount increases by £250. For every week that a child aged 10 or younger is in placement, the carer's qualifying amount increases by £200.

- If foster carers receive more than their qualifying amount they can choose whether to be taxed on the 'profit method', in which they pay tax on any profits for fostering (income received minus expenses and capital allowances) or the 'simplified method' in which they pay tax on all fostering income which exceeds the qualifying amount. The Inland Revenue has a fact sheet on the tax arrangements, www.hmrc.gov.uk/helpsheets/hs236.pdf, and can be contacted on 0845 9000 444 for advice. Advice on all tax issues for those on a low income is available from the charity TaxAid, open Monday to Friday 10am–12noon, on 0345 120 3779 and at www.taxaid.org.uk/.

Part III

The Care Standards Act 2000 (Registration) (England) Regulations 2010

The Her Majesty's Chief Inspector of Schools, Children's Services and Skills (Fees and Frequency of Inspections) (Children's Homes etc) Regulations 2007

Applications [regs.3–7 CSA 2000 (Registration) Regulations 2010]

- An application for registration must be:
  - in writing on a form approved by the CI (Her Majesty's Chief Inspector for Education, Children's Services and Skills)
  - sent or delivered to the CI
  - be accompanied by a recent photograph (which is a true likeness) of the responsible person
  - give information as required by regulation 3(2)–(4).
- An applicant to be a registered provider of a fostering agency must provide the CI with full information about the matters set out in Schedule 1, Part 1 and 2.

  Where the applicant is an individual, that information is:

  - the responsible person's full name, date of birth, current address and telephone number
  - any other addresses the responsible person has lived at within the last five years
  - the responsible person's relevant professional or technical qualifications and experience of carrying on an establishment or agency
  - the responsible person's employment history, including the name and address of their present employer and of any previous employers
  - details of any business the responsible person carries on or has carried on
  - the name and addresses of two referees who are not relatives of the responsible person and one of whom has employed the responsible person for a period of at least three months, unless this is impracticable.

  Where the applicant is a partnership, that information is:

  - the name and address of the partnership

- in relation to each member of the partnership, the information required for the registration of an individual (above).

Where the applicant is an organisation, the information is:

- the name of the organisation and the address of the principal office of the organisation
- the full name, date of birth, address and telephone number of the responsible individual
- the relevant professional or technical qualifications of the responsible individual and that individual's experience of carrying on a similar agency
- if the organisation is a subsidiary of a holding company, the name and address of the registered or principal office of the holding company and of any other subsidiary of that holding company.

In all cases except where the applicant is a local authority, the information required is:

- a reference from a bank as to the applicant's financial standing
- a statement as to whether the responsible person has been adjudged bankrupt, in respect of whom a debt relief order has been made or sequestration of his estate has been ordered, or has made a composition or arrangement with, or granted a trust deed for, their creditors
- a statement as to the applicant's ability to ensure the financial viability of the agency
- a business plan in respect of the agency
- the cash-flow or predicted cash-flow in respect of the agency.

Information about the establishment or agency:

- the name, address, telephone number, fax number, and email address of the agency
- where the agency is being operated from more than one site the name,

address, telephone number, fax number, and email address (if any) of each site

- the description of agency by reference to a description specified in section 4(8)(a) or (9)(a) of the Care Standards Act in respect of which the applicant seeks to be registered
- the statement of purpose of the agency
- a statement as to the accommodation, facilities and services which are to be provided by the agency including their extent and facilities and services at each site on which the agency operates
- where applicable, details of any travel arrangements between sites
- the date on which the agency was established or is proposed to be established
- the scale of charges payable by the service users
- in respect of each of the premises to be used by an agency
  - a description of the premises, including whether purpose-built or have been converted
  - a description of the area in which the premises are located
- a statement as to whether, at the date the application is made, the premises are capable of being used for the purpose of achieving the aims and objectives of the agency and providing appropriate facilities and services without the need for planning permission, building works, or conversion of the premises or details of the permission, works or conversion needed
- a statement as to the security arrangements, including arrangements for safeguarding access to information and restricting access from adjacent premises or from other parts of the building
- the name and address of any other agency, of a description specified in section 4(8)(a) or (9)(a) of the Act, which the applicant has or has had a business or financial interest, or at which the applicant is or has been employed, and details of such interest or employment

- whether any other business is or will be carried on in the same premises as those of the agency and, if so, details of that business.

Information about staff posts:

- a list of staff posts at the agency and the duties and responsibilities attaching to each post.

▪ The Chief Inspector may request further information about staffing of the agency.

▪ An applicant to be a registered manager of an agency must provide to the CI the information requested in Schedule 3 Part 1 and the documents listed in Part 2 [reg.3(3)] which is:

- the applicant's full name, date of birth, current address and telephone number
- any other addresses the applicant has lived at in the last five years
- the applicant's relevant professional or technical qualifications, and relevant experience of managing an agency
- the applicant's professional training relevant to carrying on or managing an agency
- the applicant's employment history, including the name and address of their present employer and of any previous employers
- details of any business the applicant carries on or manages or has carried on or managed
- the name and addresses of two referees who are not relatives of the applicant, each of whom is able to provide a reference as to the applicant's competence to manage an agency of the same description as the agency and one of whom has employed the applicant for a period of at least three months, unless impracticable
- the name, address, telephone number, fax number and email address of the agency.

Documents:

- the applicant's birth certificate
- certificates or other suitable evidence of the applicant's relevant qualifications
- a report by a general medical practitioner as to whether the applicant is physically and mentally fit to manage an agency, or if they are unable to obtain the report a statement by the applicant as to the state of her/his physical and mental health
- an enhanced criminal record certificate issued under section 113B of the Police Act 1997 and suitability information relating to children (as defined in section 113BA(2) of that Act) and the application for that certificate which was signed by the CI.

- The responsible person may be required to attend an interview to enable the CI to determine whether she/he is fit to carry on or manage the agency [reg.4].

- The applicant must give written notice to the CI of any changes to the information or documents after the application is made and before it is determined.

- Regulation 6 sets out obligations with respect to information required about staff engaged, after an application is made and before it is determined.

Register and certificate [regs.7, 8 & 9 CSA 2000 (Registration) Regulations 2010]

- The CI must maintain a register in respect of fostering agencies and other establishments specified in section 4(8)(a) and (9)(a) CSA 2000.

- Each register must contain particulars specified in Schedule 5 CSA 2000 (Registration) Regulations 2010.

- The contents of a certificate issued by the CI will contain particulars specified in regulation 8.

  If a person's registration is cancelled, she/he must, not later than the day on which the decision/order cancelling it takes effect, return it to the CI by delivering/sending it by registered post or recorded delivery [reg.9].

Conditions and reports and cancellation of registration [regs.10–13 CSA 2000 (Registration) Regulations 2010]

- Regulation 10 details the process for an application to vary or remove a condition in relation to registration.
- Regulation 11 requires the registered person to report to the CI if it appears that the agency is likely to cease to be financially viable.
- Regulations 12 &13 specify grounds for cancellation of registration (other grounds for cancellation are contained in section 14 CSA 2000).

Registration fees [reg.7 The Her Majesty's Chief Inspector of Schools, Children's Services and Skills (Fees and Frequency of Inspections)(Children's Homes etc) Regulations 2007]

- Application for registration by a person seeking to be registered as a person who carries on a fostering agency:
  - £2,186.00
- Application for registration by a person seeking to be registered as a person who manages a fostering agency:
  - £595.00

Variation fees [reg.13]

- Application under section 15(1)(a) CSA 2000 (variation or removal of any condition for time being in force in relation to the registration):
  - £1,093.00 for registered provider
- Fee for 'minor variation' (i.e. if successful, not requiring a material alteration to register of CSCI) is £99.00.

Annual fees [regs.15 & 18 (as amended by The Her Majesty's Chief Inspector of Schools, Children's Services and Skills (Fees and Frequency of Inspections)(Children's Homes etc)(Amendment) Regulations 2010]

- Annual fees for those providing fostering services:
  - Local authority service £2,185.70
  - Fostering agency £1,987.00

Frequency of inspection [reg.19]

- The CI will inspect both local authority and fostering agencies at a minimum frequency of once in every three-year period. OFSTED launched a consultation on 7 June 2011 into the inspection regime and regulations may be amended as a result.
- Any inspection may be unannounced [reg.19(3)].

Part IV

National Minimum Standards

Introduction

- The standards are applicable to local authority fostering services, independent fostering providers and voluntary organisations providing services under section 59 of the Children Act 1989.

- These set out and describe the absolute minimum standards that govern the state's expectations about how a specific service should be provided. They describe physical standards, the level of quality of service and the way in which systems and processes should be organised. They also sometimes describe the way in which the staff providing the service should behave and what qualifications they should have. The standards are underpinned by the 2011 Regulations and they help to flesh out the regulatory requirement. They are a minimum standard for providers, commissioners and users to judge the quality of a service. Inspectors must take them into account and use them as accurate descriptors when judging whether providers are compliant with regulations.

- The standards are qualitative, in that they focus on the impact on the individual of the services provided. They are also intended to be measurable and are grouped as follows:

  - Child-focused standards

  - Standards of fostering service

- Each standard is preceded by a statement of the desired outcome to be achieved by the fostering service provider and the full set of numbered paragraphs of each standard must be met in order to achieve compliance with the standards.

- Regulations to which each standard is linked are cited in the italicised paragraph and unless otherwise specified, refer to the Fostering Services (England) Regulations 2011 and the Children Act 1989 respectively.

The values statement below explains the important principles which underpin these standards.

Values

- The child's welfare, safety and needs are at the centre of their care.
- Children should have an enjoyable childhood, benefiting from excellent parenting and education, enjoying a wide range of opportunities to develop their talents and skills leading to a successful adult life.
- Children are entitled to grow up in a loving environment that can meet their developmental needs.
- Every child should have his or her wishes and feelings listened to and taken into account.
- Each child should be valued as an individual and given personalised support in line with their individual needs and background in order to develop their identity, self-confidence and self-worth.
- The particular needs of disabled children and children with complex needs will be fully recognised and taken into account.
- The significance of contact for looked after children, and of maintaining relationships with birth parents and the wider family, including siblings, half-siblings and grandparents, is recognised, as is the foster carer's role in this.
- Children in foster care deserve to be treated as a good parent would treat their own children and to have the opportunity for as full an experience of family life and childhood as possible, without unnecessary restrictions.
- The central importance of the child's relationship with their foster carer should be acknowledged and foster carers should be recognised as core members of the team working with the child.
- Foster carers have a right to full information about the child.
- It is essential that foster carers receive relevant support services and development opportunities in order to provide the best care for children.
- Genuine partnership between all those involved in fostering children is

essential for the standards to deliver the best outcomes for children; this includes the Government, local government, other statutory agencies, fostering service providers and foster carers.

Application to short breaks

Both the 2011 Regulations and the standards are modified in relation to short breaks. This is in recognition that where the child receives short breaks, the parents have primary responsibility for planning for their child. Regulation 42 defines short break care and sets out the modifications, which are that the following regulations do not apply in relation to the child where the child is on a short break: regulations 14, 15(2)(a) and (d), and 16.

The following standards do not apply in relation to short break care: standard 2.5, 2.7 and all of standards 9 and 12. In addition, there is no requirement for a separate placement plan for children looked after in a series of short breaks (Care Planning, Placement and Case Review (England) Regulations 2010, regulation 48(3)). For such children, the short break care plan includes key elements of the placement plan. Where the standards state 'placement plan', this will be the short break care plan in relation to children on short breaks.

CHILD-FOCUSED STANDARDS

STANDARD 1 – The child's wishes and feelings and the views of those significant to them

Underpinning legislation

Regulation 11 – Independent fostering agencies – duty to secure welfare
Regulation 18 – Independent fostering agencies – representations and complaints
Section 22 – General duties of local authority in relation to children looked after by them
Sections 61 and 62 – duties of voluntary organisations and local authorities

in relation to children accommodated by or on behalf of the voluntary organisation

Outcome

Children know that their views, wishes and feelings are taken into account in all aspects of their care; are helped to understand why it may not be possible to act upon their wishes in all cases; and know how to obtain support and make a complaint.
The views of others with an important relationship to the child are gathered and taken into account.

Standard

1.1 Children's views, wishes and feelings are acted upon, unless this is contrary to their interests or adversely affects other members of the foster care household.

1.2 Children understand how their views have been taken into account and where significant wishes or concerns are not acted upon, they are helped to understand why.

1.3 Children communicate their views on all aspects of their care and support.

1.4 The views of the child, the child's family, social worker and Independent Reviewing Officer are sought regularly on the child's care (unless in individual cases this is not appropriate).

1.5 Children have access to independent advice and support from adults who they can contact directly and in private about problems or concerns, which is appropriate to their age and understanding. Children know their rights to advocacy, how to access an advocate and how to contact the Children's Rights Director.

1.6 Children can take up issues in the most appropriate way with support, without fear that this will result in any adverse consequences. Children receive prompt feedback on any concerns or complaints raised and are kept informed of progress.

1.7 The wishes, feelings and views of children and those significant to them are taken into account in monitoring foster carers and developing the fostering service.

STANDARD 2 – Promoting a positive identity, potential and valuing diversity through individualised care

Underpinning legislation

Regulation 11 – Independent fostering agencies – duty to secure welfare
Section 22 – General duties of local authority in relation to children looked after by them
Sections 61 and 62 – duties of voluntary organisations and local authorities in relation to children accommodated by or on behalf of the voluntary organisation

Outcome

Children have a positive self view, emotional resilience and knowledge and understanding of their background.

Standard

2.1 Children are provided with personalised care that meets their needs and promotes all aspects of their individual identity.

2.2 Foster carers are supported to promote children's social and emotional development, and to enable children to develop emotional resilience and positive self-esteem.

2.3 Foster carers meet children's individual needs as set out in the child's placement plan as part of the wider family context.

2.4 Children exercise choice in the food that they eat, and are able to prepare their own meals and snacks, within the context of the foster family's decision making and the limits that a responsible parent would set.

2.5 Children exercise choice and independence in the clothes and personal requisites that they buy and have these needs met, within the context of the foster family's decision making and the reasonable limits that a responsible parent would set. **This sub-standard is not applicable to short break placements.**

2.6 Children develop skills and emotional resilience that will prepare them for independent living.

2.7 Children receive a personal allowance appropriate to their age and understanding, that is consistent with their placement plan. **This sub-standard is not applicable to short break placements.**

STANDARD 3 – Promoting positive behaviour and relationships

Underpinning legislation

Regulation 11 – Independent fostering agencies – duty to secure welfare
Regulation 13 – Behaviour management and absence from the foster parent's home
Regulation 17 – Foster parent to be provided with up to date information about the child including the child's care plan
Section 22 – General duties of local authority in relation to children looked after by them
Sections 61 and 62 – duties of voluntary organisations and local authorities in relation to children accommodated by or on behalf of the voluntary organisation

Outcome

Children enjoy sound relationships with their foster family, interact positively with others and behave appropriately.

Standard

3.1 Foster carers have high expectations of all of the foster children in their household.

3.2 Foster carers provide an environment and culture that promotes, models and supports positive behaviour.

3.3 Children are able to develop and practice skills to build and maintain positive relationships, be assertive and to resolve conflicts positively.

3.4 Children are encouraged to take responsibility for their behaviour in a way that is appropriate to their age and abilities.

3.5 Foster carers respect the child's privacy and confidentiality, in a manner that is consistent with good parenting.

3.6 Foster carers have positive strategies for effectively supporting children where they encounter discrimination or bullying wherever this occurs.

3.7 Foster carers receive support on how to manage their responses and feelings arising from caring for children, particularly where children display very challenging behaviour, and understand how children's previous experiences can manifest in challenging behaviour.

3.8 All foster carers receive training in positive care and control of children, including training in de-escalating problems and disputes. The fostering service has a clear written policy on managing behaviour, which includes supporting positive behaviour, de-escalation of conflicts and discipline. The fostering service's policy is made clear to the responsible authority/placing authority, child and parent/s or carers before the placement begins or, in an emergency placement, at the time of the placement.

3.9 Each foster carer is aware of all the necessary information available to the fostering service about a child's circumstances, including any significant recent events, to help the foster carer understand and predict the child's needs and behaviours and support the child within their household. The fostering service follows up with the responsible authority where all such necessary information has not been provided by the authority.

3.10 The fostering service's approach to care minimises the need for police involvement to deal with challenging behaviour and avoids criminalising children unnecessarily.

STANDARD 4 – Safeguarding children

Underpinning legislation
Regulation 11 – Independent fostering agencies – duty to secure welfare
Regulation 12 – Arrangements for the protection of children

Outcome
Children feel safe and are safe. Children understand how to protect themselves and are protected from significant harm, including neglect, abuse, and accident.

Standard
4.1 Children's safety and welfare is promoted in all fostering placements. Children are protected from abuse and other forms of significant harm (e.g. sexual or labour exploitation).

4.2 Foster carers actively safeguard and promote the welfare of foster children.

4.3 Foster carers make positive relationships with children, generate a culture of openness and trust and are aware of and alert to any signs or symptoms that might indicate a child is at risk of harm.

4.4 Foster carers encourage children to take appropriate risks as a normal part of growing up. Children are helped to understand how to keep themselves safe, including when outside of the household or when using the internet or social media.

4.5 The service implements a proportionate approach to any risk assessment.

4.6 Foster carers are trained in appropriate safe care practice, including skills to care for children who have been abused. For foster carers who offer placements to disabled children, this includes training specifically on issues affecting disabled children.

4.7 The fostering service works effectively in partnership with other agencies concerned with child protection, e.g. the responsible authority, schools, hospitals, general practitioners, etc., and does not work in isolation from them.

STANDARD 5 – Missing from care

Underpinning legislation

Regulation 13 – Behaviour management and absence from the foster parent's home

Outcome

Children rarely go missing and if they do, they return quickly.
Children who do go missing are protected as far as possible and responded to positively on their return.

Standard

5.1 The care and support provided to children minimises the risk that they will go missing and reduces the risk of harm should the child go missing.

5.2 Foster carers know and implement what the fostering service and the responsible authority's policy is in relation to children going missing.

5.3 Foster carers are aware of, and do not exceed, the measures they can take to prevent a child leaving without permission under current legislation and Government guidance.

5.4 Children who are absent from the foster home without consent, but whose whereabouts are known or thought to be known by carers or staff, are protected in line with the fostering service's written procedure.

5.5 The fostering service and foster carers take appropriate action to find children who are missing, including working alongside the police where appropriate.

5.6 If a child is absent from the fostering home and their whereabouts are not known (i.e. the child is missing), the fostering service's procedures are compatible with the local Runaway and Missing from Home and Care (RMFHC) protocols and procedures applicable to the area where each foster home is located.

5.7 Where children placed out of authority go missing, the manager of the fostering service follows the local RMFHC protocol. They also comply with, and make foster carers aware of, any other processes required by the responsible authority, specified in the individual child's care plan and in the RMFHC protocol covering the authority responsible for the child's care.

5.8 Children are helped to understand the dangers and risks of leaving the foster home without permission and are made aware of where they can access help if they consider running away.

5.9 Where a child goes missing and there is concern for their welfare, or at the request of a child who has been missing, the fostering service arranges a meeting in private between the child and the responsible authority to consider the reasons for their going missing. The fostering service considers with the responsible authority and foster carer what action should be taken to prevent the child going missing in future. Any concerns arising about the foster carer or the placement are addressed, as far as is possible, in conjunction with the responsible authority.

5.10 Written records kept by the fostering service where a child goes missing detail action taken by foster carers, the circumstances of the child's return, any reasons given by the child for running away from the foster home and any action taken in the light of those reasons. This information is shared with the responsible authority and, where appropriate, the child's parents.

STANDARD 6 – Promoting good health and wellbeing

Underpinning legislation

Regulation 15 – Health of children placed with foster parents.
Children Act 1989:
Section 22 – General duties of local authority in relation to children looked after by them
Sections 61 and 62 – duties of voluntary organisations and local authorities in relation to children accommodated by or on behalf of the voluntary organisation

Outcome

Children live in a healthy environment where their physical, emotional and psychological health is promoted and where they are able to access the services to meet their health needs.

Standard

6.1 Children's physical, emotional and social development needs are promoted.

6.2 Children understand their health needs, how to maintain a healthy lifestyle and to make informed decisions about their own health.

6.3 Children are encouraged to participate in a range of positive activities that contribute to their physical and emotional health.

6.4 Children have prompt access to doctors and other health professionals, including specialist services (in conjunction with the responsible authority), when they need these services.

6.5 Children's health is promoted in accordance with their placement plan and foster carers are clear about what responsibilities and decisions are delegated to them and where consent for medical treatment needs to be obtained.

6.6 Children's wishes and feelings are sought and taken into account in their health care, according to their understanding, and foster carers advocate on behalf of children.

6.7 Foster carers receive sufficient training on health and hygiene issues and first aid, with particular emphasis on health promotion and communicable diseases.

6.8 Foster carers receive guidance and training to provide appropriate care if looking after children with complex health needs.

6.9 Medicines kept in the foster home are stored safely and are accessible only by those for whom they are intended.

6.10 Foster carers are trained in the management and administration of medication. Prescribed medication is only given to the child for whom it was prescribed, and in accordance with the prescription. Children who wish to, and who can safely keep and take their own medication, do so.

6.11 Foster carers keep a written record of all medication, treatment and first aid given to children during their placement.

6.12 Any physical adaptations or equipment needed for the appropriate care of the children are provided to foster carers.

STANDARD 7 – Leisure activities

Underpinning legislation

Regulation 16 – Education, employment and leisure activities

Outcome

Children are able to enjoy their interests, develop confidence in their skills and are supported and encouraged to engage in leisure activities.
Children are able to make a positive contribution to the foster home and their wider community.

Standard

7.1 Children develop their emotional, intellectual, social, creative and physical skills through the accessible and stimulating environment created within the foster home. Children are supported to take part in school based and out of school activities.

7.2 Children pursue individual interests and hobbies. They take part in a range of activities, including leisure activities and trips.

7.3 Foster carers understand what is in the child's placement plan and have clarity about decisions they can make about the day to day arrangements for the child, including such matters as education, leisure activities, overnight stays, holidays, and personal issues such as hair cuts.

7.4 Foster carers are supported to make reasonable and appropriate decisions within the authority delegated to them, without having to seek consent unnecessarily.

7.5 Children have permission to take part in age appropriate peer activities as would normally be granted by a reasonable parent to their children, within the framework of the placement plan. Decision-making and any assessment of risk to the child should be undertaken on the same basis as a reasonable parent would do.

7.6 Children are encouraged and enabled to make and sustain friendships, which may involve reciprocal arrangements to visit friends' homes.

7.7 Children can stay overnight, holiday with friends, or friends and relatives of their foster carer, or go on schools trips, subject to requirements of the care/placement plan, if foster carers consider it appropriate in individual circumstances. CRB checks are not normally sought as a precondition.

STANDARD 8 – Promoting educational attainment

Underpinning legislation
Regulation 16 – Education, employment and leisure activities
Section 22(3A) – Duty on local authority to promote educational achievement

Outcome
The education and achievement of children is actively promoted as valuable in itself and as part of their preparation for adulthood. Children are supported to achieve their educational potential.

Standard
8.1 Children, including pre-school children and older children, have a foster home which promotes a learning environment and supports their development.

8.2 Children have access to a range of educational resources to support their learning and have opportunities beyond the school day to engage in activities which promote learning.

8.3 Children are supported to attend school, or alternative provision, regularly.

8.4 Children are helped by their foster carer to achieve their educational or training goals and foster carers are supported to work with a child's education provider to maximise each child's achievement and to minimise any underachievement.

8.5 The fostering service has, and is fully implementing, a written education policy that promotes and values children's education and is understood by foster carers.

8.6 Foster carers maintain regular contact with each child's school and other education settings, attending all parents' meetings as appropriate and advocating for the child where appropriate.

8.7 Foster carers engage and work with schools, colleges and other organisations to support children's education, including advocating to help overcome any problems the child may be experiencing in their education setting. Foster carers have up-to-date information about each child's educational progress and school attendance record.

STANDARD 9 – Promoting and supporting contact

Underpinning legislation
Regulation 14 – Duty to promote contact

Outcome
Children have, where appropriate, constructive contact with their parents, grandparents, siblings, half-siblings, wider family, friends and other people who play a significant role in their lives.

Standard
9.1 Children are supported and encouraged to maintain and develop family contacts and friendships, subject to any limitations or provisions set out in their care plan and any court order.

9.2 Foster carers are given practical help to support appropriate contact, including financial help where needed, alongside support to manage any difficult emotional or other issues that the child and foster carer may have as a result of contact.

9.3 Emergency restrictions on contact are only made to protect the child from significant risk to their safety or welfare and are communicated to the responsible authority within 24 hours of being imposed.

9.4 Ongoing restriction on communication by the child is agreed by the child's responsible authority, takes the child's wishes and feelings into account and is regularly reviewed in collaboration with the responsible authority.

9.5 The fostering service feeds back to the responsible authority any significant reactions a child has to contact arrangements or visits with any person.

9.6 When deciding whether to offer a placement, the fostering service works with the responsible authority in giving consideration to how the child's contact with family and significant others will be supported, particularly where a child is placed at a distance from home.

9.7 Foster carers understand what decisions about contact are delegated to them, in line with the child's care plan, and make those decisions in the child's best interests.

The above standards are not required for short breaks. For children in short breaks the foster carer must know how to contact parents and maintain such contact as has been agreed in the short break care plan

STANDARD 10 - Providing a suitable physical environment for the foster child

Underpinning legislation

Regulation 26 – Assessment of prospective foster parents
Schedule 3 – Information as to prospective foster parent and other members of their household and family

Outcome

Children live in foster homes which provide adequate space, to a suitable standard. The child enjoys access to a range of activities which promote his or her development.

Standard

10.1 The foster home can comfortably accommodate all who live there including where appropriate any suitable aids and adaptations provided and fitted by suitably trained staff when caring for a disabled child.

10.2 The foster home is warm, adequately furnished and decorated, is maintained to a good standard of cleanliness and hygiene and is in good order throughout. Outdoor spaces which are part of the premises are safe, secure and well maintained.

10.3 Foster carers are trained in health and safety issues and have guidelines on their health and safety responsibilities. Avoidable hazards are removed as is consistent with a family home.

10.4 Foster carers understand the service's policy concerning safety for children in the foster home and in vehicles used to transport foster children. The service's policy is regularly reviewed in line with the most recent guidance from relevant bodies.

10.5 The foster home is inspected annually, without appointment, by the fostering service to make sure that it continues to meet the needs of foster children.

10.6 In the foster home, each child over the age of three should have their own bedroom. If this is not possible, the sharing of a bedroom is agreed by each child's responsible authority and each child has their own area within the bedroom. Before seeking agreement for the sharing of a bedroom, the fostering service provider takes into account any potential for bullying, any history of abuse or abusive behaviour, the wishes of the children concerned and all other pertinent facts. The decision making process and outcome of the assessment are recorded in writing where bedroom sharing is agreed.

STANDARD 11 – Preparation for a placement

Underpinning legislation

Regulation 11 – Independent fostering agencies – duty to secure welfare
Section 22 – General duty of local authority in relation to children looked after by them
CPPR 2010 Regulation 22 – Conditions to be complied with before placing a child with a local authority foster parent

Outcome

Children are welcomed into the foster home and leave the foster home in a planned and sensitive manner which makes them feel loved and valued. Children feel part of the family. They are not treated differently to the foster carer's own children living in the household. The child's needs are met and they benefit from a stable placement.

Standard

11.1 The service has and implements clear procedures for introducing children into the foster care placement, to the foster carer and to others living in the household, which cover planned and, where permitted, emergency/immediate foster care placements. They help children understand what to expect from living in the foster home.

11.2 Children are carefully matched to a foster placement. Foster carers have full information about the child (as set out in standard 3.9).

11.3 Unless an emergency placement makes it impossible, children are given information about the foster carer before arrival, and any information (including where appropriate, photographic information) they need or reasonably request about the placement, in a format appropriate to their age and understanding. Wherever possible, children are able to visit the foster carer's home and to talk with the foster carers in private prior to a placement decision being made. Children can bring their favourite possessions into the foster carer's home.

11.4 Children are given free access to the household facilities as would be consistent with reasonable arrangements in a family home. Foster carers explain everyday household rules and expectations to children.

11.5 Where children are leaving the foster family, they are helped to understand the reasons why they are leaving. Children are supported during the transition to their new placement, to independent living or to their parental home.

11.6 Foster carers are supported to maintain links with children moving on, consistent with their care plan.

STANDARD 12 – Promoting independence and moves to adulthood and leaving care

Underpinning legislation

Regulation 11 – Independent fostering agencies – duty to secure welfare
Section 22 – General duty of local authority in relation to children looked after by them

Outcome

Children are prepared for, and supported into, adulthood so that they can reach their potential and achieve economic wellbeing.

Standard

12.1 Children are supported to:

a) establish positive and appropriate social and sexual relationships;
b) develop positive self-esteem and emotional resilience;
c) prepare for the world of work and or further or higher education;
d) prepare for moving into their own accommodation;
e) develop practical skills, including shopping, buying, cooking and keeping food, washing clothes, personal self-care, and understanding and taking responsibility for personal healthcare;
f) develop financial capability, knowledge and skills;
g) know about entitlements to financial and other support after leaving care, including benefits and support from social care services.

12.2 Foster carers contribute to the development of each child's care plan, in collaboration with the child, including the pathway plan for an 'eligible' child, and work collaboratively with the young person's social worker or personal adviser in implementing the plan.

12.3 The fostering service ensures there are comprehensive arrangements for preparing and supporting young people to make the transition to independence. This includes appropriate training and support to foster carers caring for young people who are approaching adulthood. Arrangements are consistent with the young person's care plan, including their placement plan, pathway plan and transition plan for children with disabilities and special educational needs.

12.4 The fostering service has a policy and practical arrangements which enable children to remain with their foster carer(s) into legal adulthood, for example so that s/he may develop appropriate life skills before being required to move to more independent accommodation. Any such decisions are agreed with foster carers at a placement meeting and are detailed in a child's placement plan.

The above standards are not required for short breaks.

STANDARDS OF FOSTERING SERVICE

STANDARD 13 – Recruiting and assessing foster carers who can meet the needs of looked after children

---

Underpinning legislation

Regulation 26 – Assessment of prospective foster parents
Regulation 27 – Approval of foster parents
Regulation 28 – Reviews and terminations of approval
Section 22G – General duty of local authority to secure sufficient accommodation for looked after children

Outcome

The fostering service recruits, assesses and supports a range of foster carers to meet the needs of children they provide care for and is proactive in assessing current and future needs of children.

Standard

13.1 The local authority fostering service implements an effective strategy to ensure sufficient foster carers to be responsive to current and predicted future demands on the service. Planning for future demands covers the need for short breaks for disabled children.

13.2 People who are interested in becoming foster carers are treated fairly, without prejudice, openly and with respect. Enquiries are dealt with courteously and efficiently by staff who have the necessary knowledge and skills. Prospective foster carers are provided with timely and relevant information following their initial enquiry and are kept informed about the progress of any subsequent application for approval.

13.3 Prospective foster carers are prepared to become foster carers in a way which addresses, and gives practical techniques to manage, the issues they are likely to encounter and identifies the competencies and strengths they have or need to develop.

13.4 The assessment process is set out clearly to prospective foster carers, including:

a) the qualities, skills or aptitudes being sought or to be achieved;
b) the standards to be applied in the assessment;
c) the stages and content of the selection process and where possible timescales involved;
d) the information to be given to applicants.

13.5 Checks are carried out in line with regulation 26 and prospective foster carers understand why identity checks, relationship status and health checks, personal references and enquiries are undertaken about them and why enhanced CRB checks are made on them and adult members of their household.

13.6 Prospective foster carers are considered in terms of their capacity to look after children in a safe and responsible way that meets the child's development needs.

13.7 The written report on the person's suitability to be approved as a foster carer sets out clearly all the information that the fostering panel and decision maker needs in order to make an objective approval decision. The reports are accurate, up-to-date and include evidence based information that distinguishes between fact, opinion and third party information. The reports are prepared, signed and dated by the social worker who assessed the prospective foster carer and countersigned and dated by the fostering team manager or a team manager of another of the provider's fostering teams.

13.8 Reviews of foster carers' approval are sufficiently thorough to allow the fostering service to properly satisfy itself about their carers' ongoing suitability to foster.

13.9 Areas of concern, or need for additional support, that are identified between reviews are addressed. Such matters identified between reviews are addressed at the time they are identified, where appropriate, rather than waiting for a review.

STANDARD 14 – Fostering panels and the fostering service's decision-maker

Underpinning legislation

Regulation 23 – Constitution and membership of fostering panel
Regulation 24 – Meetings of fostering panel
Regulation 26 – Assessment of prospective foster parents
Regulation 27 – Approval of foster parents
Regulation 28 – Reviews and terminations of approval

Outcome

The fostering panel and decision maker make timely, quality and appropriate recommendations/decisions in line with the overriding objective to promote the welfare of children in foster care.

Standard

14.1 The fostering service implements clear written policies and procedures on recruitment to, and maintenance of, the central list of persons considered by them to be suitable to be members of a fostering panel ('the central list') and on constitution of fostering panels.

14.2 Panel/s provide a quality assurance feedback to the fostering service provider on the quality of reports being presented to panel.

14.3 All necessary information is provided to panel members at least five working days in advance of the panel meeting to enable full and proper consideration.

14.4 The fostering panel makes its recommendation on the suitability of a prospective foster carer within eight months of receipt of the prospective foster carer's application to be assessed.

14.5 Foster carers and prospective foster carers are given the opportunity to attend and be heard at all panel meetings at which their approval is being discussed and to bring a supporter to the panel if they wish.

14.6 Fostering panels have access to medical expertise and legal advice, as required.

14.7 The panel chair ensures written minutes of panel meetings are accurate and clearly cover the key issues and views expressed by panel members and record the reasons for its recommendation.

14.8 The number, skills, knowledge and experience of persons on the central list are sufficient to enable the fostering service to constitute panels that are equipped to make competent recommendations to the fostering service provider, taking into account the nature of the children and carers that the service caters for.

14.9 The fostering service provider's decision-maker makes a considered decision that takes account of all the information available to them, including the recommendation of the fostering panel and, where applicable, the independent review panel, within seven working days of receipt of the recommendation and final set of panel minutes.

14.10 The foster carer or prospective foster carer is informed orally of the decision-maker's decision within two working days and written confirmation is sent to them within five working days.

STANDARD 15 – Matching the child with a placement that meets their assessed needs

Underpinning legislation

Regulation 17 – Support, training and information for foster parents
CPPR 2010 Regulation 9 – Placement plan
Regulation 14 – Termination of placement by the responsible authority

Outcome

The responsible authority has information and support from the fostering service which it needs to facilitate an appropriate match between the carer and child, capable of meeting the child's needs and consistent with the wishes and feelings of the child, so maximising the likelihood of a stable placement.

Standard

15.1 The fostering service only suggests foster carers to local authorities as a potential match for a child if the foster carer can reasonably be expected to meet the child's assessed needs and the impact of the placement on existing household members has been considered. Where gaps are identified, the fostering service should work with the responsible authority to ensure the placement plan sets out any additional training, resource or support required.

15.2 Prior to the placement of each child, the foster carer is provided with all the information held by the fostering service that they need to carry out their role effectively. The information is provided in a clear, comprehensive written form and includes the support that will be available to the foster carer. The fostering service follows up with the responsible authority any gaps in the information provided to them on the child or the child's family, which may hinder the foster carer in providing a safe caring environment that meets the child's needs and enables them to keep the child, other children in the fostering household and the foster carer him/ herself safe.

15.3 Once placed, a child is not removed from a foster carer who is willing and able to continue caring for the child, unless that is in their best interests, taking the child's current wishes and feelings into account, and decided (other than in an emergency) through the child's care planning process. If a placement move occurs in an emergency the fostering service informs the responsible authority within one working day.

STANDARD 16 – Statement of purpose and children's guide

Underpinning legislation

Regulation 3 – Statement of purpose and children's guide
Regulation 4 – Review of statement of purpose and children's guide

Outcome

Children, their parents, foster carers, staff and the responsible authority/ placing authority are clear about the aims and objectives of the fostering service and what services and facilities it provides.
The fostering services operation meets the aims and objectives in the Statement of Purpose.

Standard

16.1 The fostering service has a clear statement of purpose which is available to, and understood by, foster carers, staff and children and is reflected in any policies, procedures and guidance. It is available to the responsible authority and any parent or person with parental responsibility.

16.2 The aims and objectives of the Statement of Purpose are child focused and show how the service will meet outcomes for children.

16.3 Subject to the child's age and understanding, the fostering service ensures the child receives the Children's Guide at the point of placement and that the foster carer explains the contents of the Children's Guide in a way that is accessible.

16.4 The Children's Guide includes a summary of what the fostering service sets out to do for children, how they can find out their rights, how a child can contact their Independent Reviewing Officer, the Children's Rights Director, Ofsted if they wish to raise a concern with inspectors, and how to secure access to an independent advocate.

16.5 Where a child requires it, the guide is available, where appropriate, through suitable alternative methods of communication, e.g. Makaton, pictures, tape recording, translation into another language.

STANDARD 17 - Fitness to provide or manage the administration of a fostering service

Underpinning legislation

Regulation 5 – Fostering agency – fitness of fostering service provider
Regulation 6 – Fostering agency – appointment of manager
Regulation 7 – Fostering agency – fitness of manager
Regulation 8 – Fostering agency – Registered person – general requirements
Regulation 10 – Local authority fostering service – manager

Outcome

The fostering service is provided and managed by those who are suitable to work with children and have the appropriate skills, experience and qualifications to deliver an efficient and effective service.

Standard

17.1 People involved in carrying on and managing the fostering service:

a) have good knowledge and experience of law and practice relating to looked after children;
b) have business and management skills to manage the work efficiently and effectively; and
c) have financial expertise to ensure that the fostering service is run on a sound financial basis and in a professional manner.

17.2 The registered manager (or registered person, where the registered person is an individual and there is no registered manager) has:

a) a recognised social work qualification or a professional qualification relevant to working with children at least at level 4;*
b) a qualification in management at least at level 4;*
c) at least two years' experience relevant to fostering within the last five years; and
d) at least one years' experience supervising and managing professional staff.

17.3 Appointees to the role of registered manager who do not have the management qualification (above) must enrol on a management training course within six months, and obtain a relevant management qualification within three years, of their appointment.

17.4 The responsibilities and duties of the manager, and to whom they are accountable, are clear and understood by them. The manager is notified in writing of any change in the person to whom they are accountable.

---

* With respect to standard 17.2 (a) and (b), for persons undertaking a qualification after January 2011, the relevant qualification will be the Level 5 Diploma in Leadership for Health and Social Care and Children and Young People's Services. Managers who already hold a Level 4 Leadership and Management for Care Services and Health and Social Care will not need to undertake this qualification at Level 5.

17.5 The manager exercises effective leadership of the staff and operation, such that the fostering service is organised, managed and staffed in a manner that delivers the best possible child care that meets the individual needs of each fostered child and of foster carers.

STANDARD 18 – Financial viability and changes affecting business continuity

Underpinning legislation

Regulation 33 – Fostering agency ceasing to carry out fostering functions – notifications and records
Regulation 34 – Fostering agency ceasing to carry out fostering functions – new fostering service providers
Regulation 37 – Financial position
Regulation 38 – Notice of absence
Regulation 39 – Notice of changes
Regulation 40 – Appointment of liquidators

Outcome

The fostering service is financially sound.
Where a service is to close or substantially change, there is proper planning, to make the transition for children, foster carers and staff as smooth as possible.

Standard

18.1 A qualified accountant certifies that the independent fostering agency's annual accounts indicate the service is financially viable and likely to have sufficient funding to continue to fulfil its Statement of Purpose for at least the next 12 months.

18.2 The registered provider has a written development plan, reviewed annually, for the future of the service, either identifying any planned changes in the operation or resources of the service, or confirming the continuation of the service's current operation and resource.

18.3 Where the service, for any reason, cannot adequately and consistently maintain provision which complies with regulations or NMS, an effective plan must be established and implemented either to rectify the situation or to close down the service.

18.4 The registered provider must notify Ofsted, the responsible authority and where different the placing authority, if closure of the service or substantial change to the service significantly affecting the care, welfare or placement of children, is likely or actively being considered. The registered person should work with the responsible authority/placing authority to ensure as smooth a transition for children and foster carers as possible.

18.5 Any person or organisation temporarily responsible for a fostering service in administration or receivership, or in the process of closure or substantial change, must operate the service in the best interests of the placed children and foster carers under the circumstances that apply, in accordance with the applicable regulations and these standards.

STANDARD 19 - Suitability to work with children

Underpinning legislation

Regulation 20 – Fitness of workers
Regulation 21 – Employment of staff
Regulation 22 – Records with respect to fostering services
Regulation 30 – Case records relating to foster parents and others

Outcome

There is careful selection of staff, fostering households, volunteers and the central list of persons considered suitable to be members of a fostering panel, and there is monitoring of such people to help prevent unsuitable people from having the opportunity to harm children.

Standard

19.1 All people working in or for the fostering service, and the central list of persons considered suitable to be members of a fostering panel, are interviewed as part of the selection process and have references checked to assess suitability before taking on responsibilities. Telephone enquiries are made to each referee to verify the written references.*

19.2 The fostering service can demonstrate, including from written records, that it consistently follows good recruitment practice, and all applicable current statutory requirements and guidance, in foster carer selection and staff and panel member recruitment. This includes CRB checks.** All personnel responsible for recruitment and selection of staff are trained in, understand and operate these good practices.

19.3 The fostering service has a record of the recruitment and suitability checks which have been carried out for foster carers and those working (including as volunteers) for the fostering service which includes:

a) identity checks;
b) CRB Disclosures, including the level of the Disclosure, and the unique reference number (in line with eligibility to obtain such checks);
c) checks to confirm qualifications which are a requirement and those that are considered by the fostering service to be relevant;
d) at least two references, preferably one from a current employer, and where possible a statement from each referee as to their opinion of the person's suitability to work with children;
e) checks to confirm the right to work in the UK;
f) where the person has lived outside of the UK, further checks, as are considered appropriate, where obtaining a CRB Disclosure is not sufficient to establish suitability to work with children.

19.4 The record must show the date on which each check was completed and who carried out the check. The CRB Disclosure information must be kept

---

* These requirements are the responsibility of Ofsted with respect to checking suitability of those seeking to carry on or manage a fostering service.

** Please note that the Government is currently reviewing the criminal records system and vetting and barring scheme and therefore references in both the Regulations and Standards may be subject to change.

in secure conditions and be destroyed by secure means as soon as it is no longer needed in line with the CRB Code of Practice. Before the Disclosure is destroyed, records need to be kept as described above.

19.5 The registered person's system for recruiting staff and others includes an effective system for reaching decisions as to who is to be appointed and the circumstances in which an application should be refused in the light of any criminal convictions or other concerns about suitability that are declared or discovered through the recruitment process.

19.6 There is a whistle-blowing policy which is made known to all staff, volunteers, foster carers and panel members. This makes it a clear duty for such people to report to an appropriate authority any circumstances within the fostering service which they consider likely to significantly harm the safety, rights or welfare of any child placed by the service.

STANDARD 20 – Learning and development of foster carers

Underpinning legislation

Regulation 17 – Support, training and information for foster parents
Regulation 28 – Reviews and terminations of approval

Outcome

Foster carers receive the training and development they need to carry out their role effectively.
A clear framework of training and development is in place and this is used as the basis for assessing foster carers' performance and identifying their training and development needs.

Standard

20.1 All new foster carers receive an induction.

20.2 All foster carers, including all members of a household who are approved foster carers, are supported to achieve the Children's Workforce

Development Council's Training, Support and Development Standards for Foster Care.* Short break carers who are approved foster carers are supported to achieve the Training Support & Development Standards for Short Break Carers. Family and friends foster carers are supported to achieve the Training, Support and Development Standards for Family and Friends Foster Carers.**

20.3 Foster carers are able to evidence that the Training, Support and Development Standards have been attained within 12 months of approval (or within 18 months for family and friends foster carers). For foster carers who were approved as such before April 2008, the standards are attained by April 2011 (or by April 2012 for family and friends foster carers). Fostering households may use the same evidence workbook.

20.4 Foster carers maintain an ongoing training and development portfolio which demonstrates how they are meeting the skills required of them by the fostering service.

20.5 Foster carers' personal development plans set out how they will be supported to undertake ongoing training and development that is appropriate to their development needs and experience.

20.6 The reviews of each carer's approval include an appraisal of performance against clear and consistent standards set by the agency, and consideration of training and development needs, which are documented in the review report. The foster carer's personal development plan is reviewed and the effectiveness of training and development received is evaluated. Reviews take into account the views of each child currently placed with the foster carer.

---

* For information and guidance please visit www.cwdcouncil.org.uk/foster-care/standards.

** Short break carers/family and friends carers may choose to undertake the mainstream Training, Support and Development Standards for Foster Care, instead of the Standards for Short Break Carers/Family and Friends Carers, if this is their preference.

20.7 The fostering service is clear and transparent with their foster carers about the level of support available to them and how to access such support.

20.8 Support and training is made available to foster carers, including hard to reach carers,* to assist them in meeting the specific needs of the children they are caring for or are expected to care for.

20.9 Appropriate training on safer caring is provided for all members of the foster household, including young people of sufficient age and understanding, and ensures that foster carers understand how safer caring principles should be applied in a way which meets the needs of individual children.

20.10 All training fits within a framework of equal opportunities and anti-discriminatory practice and is organised to encourage and facilitate attendance by foster carers.

20.11 In cases where a foster carer moves to a new fostering service, details of the development and training which he or she has undertaken, and of the extent to which the agreed training and development standards have been met, are made available on request to the new provider, and the foster carer is able to take their training and development portfolio with them.

STANDARD 21 – Supervision and support of foster carers

Underpinning legislation

Regulation 17 – Support, training and information for foster parents

Outcome

Foster carers receive the support and supervision they need in order to care properly for children placed with them.

* www.cwdcouncil.org.uk/foster-care/case-studies/reaching-all-carers provides helpful case studies.

Standard

21.1 The fostering service supports their foster carers to ensure they provide foster children with care that reasonably meets those children's needs, takes the children's wishes and feelings into account, actively promotes individual care and supports the children's safety, health, enjoyment, education and preparation for the future.

21.2 The fostering service ensures foster carers understand the nature and level of support which will be provided to them by the fostering service.

21.3 There is an effective out of hours advice and support service for foster carers.

21.4 Peer support, foster care associations and/or self help groups for foster carers are encouraged and supported.

21.5 Foster carers are provided with breaks from caring as appropriate. These are planned to take account of the needs of any children placed.

21.6 All foster carers have access to adequate social work and other professional support, information and advice, to enable them to provide consistent, high quality care to the child. This includes assistance with dealing with relevant services, such as health and education. Consideration is given to any help or support needed by the sons and daughters of foster carers.

21.7 The role of the supervising social worker is clear both to the worker and the foster carer.

21.8 Each approved foster carer is supervised by a named, appropriately qualified social worker who has meetings with the foster carer, including at least one unannounced visit a year. Meetings have a clear purpose and provide the opportunity to supervise the foster carer's work, ensure the foster carer is meeting the child's needs, taking into account the child's wishes and feelings, and offer support and a framework to assess the carer's performance and develop their competencies and skills. The frequency of meetings for short break foster carers should be proportionate to the amount of care provided. Foster carers' files include records of supervisory meetings.

21.9 The supervising social worker ensures each foster carer he or she supervises is informed in writing of, and accepts, understands and operates within, all regulations and standards and with policies and guidance agreed by the fostering service.

21.10 On approval, foster carers are given information, either a handbook or electronic resources, which cover policies, procedures (including with regard to allegations), guidance, financial information, legal information and insurance details. This information is updated regularly.

21.11 Current and prospective foster carers are able to make a complaint about any aspect of the service which affects them directly. Records are kept of representations and complaints, how they are dealt with, the outcome and any action taken. These records are reviewed regularly so that the service's practice is improved where necessary.

21.12 There is a good system of communication between the fostering service social workers and the child's social worker. The fostering service social workers understand the role of the child's social worker and work effectively with them.

STANDARD 22 – Handling allegations and suspicions of harm

Underpinning legislation

Regulation 11 – Independent fostering agencies – duty to secure welfare
Regulation 12 – Arrangements for the protection of children
Regulation 17 – Support, training and information for foster parents
Regulation 30 – Case records relating to foster carers and others
Regulation 36 – Notifiable events
Section 22 – General duties of local authority in relation to children looked after by them

Sections 61 and 62 – Duties of voluntary organisations and local authorities in relation to children accommodated by or on behalf of the voluntary organisation

Outcome

Allegations and suspicions of harm are handled in a way that provides effective protection and support for children and the person making the allegation, and at the same time supports the person who is the subject of the allegation.

Standard

22.1 All foster carers, fostering service staff and volunteers understand what they must do if they receive an allegation or have suspicions that a person may have:

a) behaved in a way that has, or may have, harmed a child;
b) possibly committed a criminal offence against or related to a child; or
c) behaved towards a child in a way that indicates he or she is unsuitable to work with children.

The fostering service ensures that the required actions are taken, or have been taken, in any relevant situation of which it is aware.

22.2 The fostering service's procedure is in line with Government guidance and requirements, including the duty to refer information to statutory bodies.* It is known to foster carers, fostering service staff, volunteers and children.

22.3 A copy of the fostering service provider's child protection procedures is made available to foster carers, fostering service staff, volunteers and children. Any comments on these procedures are taken into account by the provider.

---

* Since October 2009, the duties to refer concerns regarding individuals under List 99 and the Protection of Children Act 1999 have been replaced by a duty to provide information to the Independent Safeguarding Authority. Please see the referrals page of www.isa-gov.org.uk for information on the legal requirements for making referrals.

22.4 The fostering service provider's child protection procedures are submitted for consideration and comment to the Local Safeguarding Children's Board (LSCB) and to the Local Authority Designated Officer (LADO) for Child Protection* (or other senior officer responsible for child protection matters in that department). They are consistent with the local policies and procedures agreed by the LSCB relevant to the geographical area where the foster carer lives. Any conflicts between locally agreed procedures and those of other placing authorities are discussed and resolved as far as possible.

22.5 Each fostering service has a designated person, who is a senior manager, responsible for managing allegations. The designated person has responsibility for liaising with the LADO and for keeping the subject of the allegation informed of progress during and after the investigation.

22.6 Allegations against people that work with children or members of the fostering household are reported by the fostering service to the LADO. This includes allegations that on the face of it may appear relatively insignificant or that have also been reported directly to the police or Children and Family Services.

22.7 A clear and comprehensive summary of any allegations made against a particular member of the fostering household, or staff member, including details of how the allegation was followed up and resolved, a record of any action taken and the decisions reached, is kept on the person's confidential file. A copy is provided to the person as soon as the investigation is concluded. The information is retained on the confidential file, even after someone leaves the organisation, until the person reaches normal retirement age, or for ten years if this is longer.

22.8 As soon as possible after an investigation into a foster carer is concluded, their approval as suitable to foster is reviewed. There is a clear policy framework which outlines the circumstances in which a foster carer should be removed as one of the fostering service provider's approved foster

---

* *Working Together to Safeguard Children* (2010)

carers, in the interests of the safety or welfare of children. This is available to foster carers.

22.9 Investigations into allegations or suspicions of harm are handled fairly, quickly, and consistently in a way that provides effective protection for the child, and at the same time supports the person who is the subject of the allegation. Fostering services follow the framework for managing cases of allegations of abuse against people who work with children as set out in *Working Together to Safeguard Children*.

22.10 Fostering services ensure that a clear distinction is made between investigation into allegations of harm and discussions over standards of care. Investigations which find no evidence of harm should not become procedures looking into poor standards of care – these should be treated separately.

22.11 There is written guidance for foster carers and staff, which makes clear how they will be supported during an investigation into an allegation including payment of allowance and any fee to foster carers while investigations are ongoing.

22.12 During an investigation the fostering service makes support, which is independent of the fostering service, available to the person subject to the allegation and, where this is a foster carer, to their household, in order to provide:

a) information and advice about the process;
b) emotional support; and,
c) if needed, mediation between the foster carer and the fostering service and/or advocacy (including attendance at meetings and panel hearings).

STANDARD 23 – Learning, development and qualifications of staff

Underpinning legislation

Regulation 19 – Staffing of fostering service

Outcome

Children and foster carers receive a service from staff, volunteers and panel members and decision makers who have the competence to meet their needs.

Standard

23.1 There is a good quality learning and development programme, which includes induction, post-qualifying and in-service training, that staff and volunteers are supported to undertake. The programme equips them with the skills required to meet the needs of the children, keeps them up-to-date with professional, legal and practice developments and reflects the policies, legal obligations and business needs of the fostering service.

23.2 The learning and development programme is evaluated for effectiveness at least annually and is updated where necessary.

23.3 New staff and volunteers undertake the Children's Workforce Development Council's induction standards, commencing within 7 working days of starting their employment and being completed within six months.

23.4 All social workers and other specialists (e.g. medical, legal, educationalists, psychologists, therapists) are professionally qualified and, where applicable, registered by the appropriate professional body. They are appropriately trained to work with children, their families and foster carers, and have a good understanding of foster care and the policies and purpose of the fostering service.

23.5 Assessment and appraisal of all staff involved in fostering work takes account of identified skills needed for particular roles and is used to identify individuals' learning and development needs.

23.6 Any staff involved in assessing the suitability of persons to be foster carers are social workers, have experience of foster care and family placement work and are trained in assessment. Social work students and social workers who do not have the relevant experience, only carry out assessments under the supervision of an appropriately experienced social worker, who takes responsibility for the assessment.

23.7 Where unqualified staff and volunteers carry out social work functions they do so under the direct supervision of experienced social workers, who are accountable for their work.

23.8 Persons joining the central list of persons considered suitable to be fostering panel members are provided with an opportunity to observe a fostering panel meeting.

23.9 Each person on the central list is given induction training which is completed within 10 weeks of joining the central list.

23.10 Each person on the central list is given the opportunity of attending an annual joint training day with the fostering service's fostering staff.

23.11 Each person on the central list has access to appropriate training and skills development and is kept abreast of relevant changes to legislation and guidance.

23.12 The fostering service's decision-maker is a senior person within the fostering service, or is a trustee or director of the fostering service, who is a social worker with at least 3 years post-qualifying experience in childcare social work and has knowledge of childcare law and practice.

STANDARD 24 – Staff support and supervision

Underpinning legislation

Regulation 19 – Staffing of fostering service
Regulation 20 – Fitness of workers

Outcome

Staff and volunteers are supported and guided to fulfil their roles and provide a high quality service to children.

Standard

24.1 The employer is fair and competent, with sound employment practices and good support for all its staff and volunteers.

24.2 All staff, volunteers and the registered person are properly managed and supported and understand to whom they are accountable.

24.3 Suitable arrangements exist for professional supervision of the agency's registered person or manager of a local authority fostering service.

24.4 Staff have access to support and advice, and are provided with regular supervision by appropriately qualified and experienced staff.

24.5 A written record is kept by the fostering service detailing the time, date and length of each supervision held for each member of staff, including the registered person. The record is signed by the supervisor and the member of staff at the end of the supervision.

24.6 All staff have their performance individually and formally appraised at least annually and, where they are working with children, this appraisal takes into account any views of children the service is providing for.

24.7 Staff and volunteers are able to access the specialist advice needed to provide a comprehensive service for children, including legal advice.

STANDARD 25 – Managing effectively and efficiently and monitoring the service

Underpinning legislation

Regulation 8 – Fostering agency – Registered person – general requirements
Regulation 10 – Local authority fostering service – Manager

Regulation 18 – Independent fostering agencies – representations and complaints
Regulation 35 – Review of quality of care
Regulation 36 – Notifiable events
Regulation 37 – Financial position

Outcome
The fostering service is managed ethically, effectively and efficiently, delivering a service which meets the needs of its users.

Standard
25.1 There are clear and effective procedures for monitoring and controlling the activities of the service. This includes the financial viability of the service, any serious incidents, allegations or complaints about the service and ensuring the quality of the service.

25.2 The manager regularly monitors all records kept by the service to ensure compliance with the service's policies, to identify any concerns about specific incidents and to identify patterns and trends. Immediate action is taken to address any issues raised by this monitoring.

25.3 Management of the service ensures all staff's work and all fostering activity is consistent with the 2011 Regulations and NMS and with the service's policies and procedures.

25.4 Managers, staff, volunteers and foster carers are clear about their roles and responsibilities. The level of delegation and responsibility of the manager, and the lines of accountability, are clearly defined.

25.5 Clear arrangements are in place to identify the person in charge when the registered manager, or local authority fostering service manager, is absent.

25.6 The registered person ensures copies of inspection reports by Ofsted are made available to all members of staff, to their foster carers, children fostered by the service and their parents/carers, and, on request, to the responsible, or where different placing, authorities of existing foster children or those considering placing a child through the service.

25.7 The executive side of the local authority or the independent foster service's provider/trustees, board members or management committee members:

a) receive written reports on the management, outcomes and financial state of the fostering service every 3 months;
b) monitor the management and outcomes of the services in order to satisfy themselves that the service is effective and is achieving good outcomes for children;
c) satisfy themselves that the provider is complying with the conditions of registration.

25.8 The registered person takes action to address any issues of concern that they identify or which are raised with them.

25.9 Staff, volunteers and foster carers have a copy of:

a) the policies and working practices in respect of grievances and disciplinary matters;
b) details of the services offered;
c) the equal opportunities policy;
d) health and safety procedures.

25.10 Information is provided to commissioners of services as part of tendering. This includes:

a) charges for each of its services;
b) statements of the amounts paid to foster carers (separated by fee and allowance); and
c) any amounts paid for other services, e.g. health and education.

25.11 The registered person has provided the service with a written policy and procedural guidelines on considering and responding to representations and complaints in accordance with legal requirements and relevant statutory guidance.

25.12 The service has the facilities to work with children with physical, sensory and learning impairments, communication difficulties or for whom English is not their first language. Oral and written communications are made available in a format which is appropriate to the physical, sensory and learning impairments, communication difficulties and language of the individual. The procedures include arrangements for reading, translating, Makaton, pictures, tape recording and explaining documents to those people who are unable to understand the document.

STANDARD 26 - Records

Underpinning legislation

Regulation 22 – Records with respect to fostering services
Regulation 26 – Assessment of prospective foster parents
Regulation 30 – Case records relating to foster carers and others
Regulation 31 – Register of foster carers
Regulation 32 – Retention and confidentiality of records
Regulation 33 – Fostering agency ceasing to carry out fostering functions – notifications and records

Outcome:

Records are clear, up to date, stored securely and contribute to an understanding of the child's life.

Standard

26.1 The fostering service has and implements a written policy that clarifies the purpose, format and content of information to be kept on the fostering service's files, on the child's files and on case files relating to foster carers.

26.2 Staff, volunteers, panel members and fostering households understand the nature of records maintained and follow the service's policy for the keeping and retention of files, managing confidential information and access to files (including files removed from the premises). There is a system in place to monitor the quality and adequacy of record keeping and take action when needed.

26.3 Children and their parents understand the nature of records maintained and how to access them.

26.4 Information about individual children is kept confidential and only shared with those who have a legitimate and current need to know the information, and to those parts of a child's record or other information that they need to know.

26.5 Entries in records, decisions and reasons for them, are legible, clearly expressed, non-stigmatising, distinguish between fact, opinion and third party information and are signed and dated.

26.6 Information about the child is recorded clearly and in a way which will be helpful to the child when they access their files now or in the future. Children are actively encouraged to read their files, other than necessarily confidential or third party information, and to correct errors and add personal statements.

26.7 The foster carer understands the important supporting role they play in encouraging the child to reflect on and understand their history. The child, subject to age and understanding, is encouraged to keep appropriate memorabilia (including photographs) of their time in the placement. The fostering service makes this role clear to their foster carers and ensures they can record, and help children make a record of (subject to age and understanding), significant life events.

26.8 Where there is an agency placement, the agency works with the responsible authority to ensure effective integration of information held in the agency's case files and those of the responsible authority. On receipt of a written request by a child's responsible authority, the agency immediately provides copies of records and documents in relation to the child.

26.9 When a foster carer seeks to move to a new provider, the new provider seeks information from the previous provider about the prospective foster carer, and the previous provider complies with such a request within one month of receipt of the written request.

STANDARD 27 – Fitness of premises for use as fostering service

Underpinning legislation

Regulation 32 – Retention and confidentiality of records

Outcome

The premises and administrative systems are suitable to enable the service to meet the objectives of its Statement of Purpose.

Standard

27.1 There are efficient and robust administrative systems, including IT and communication systems. Premises have:

a) facilities for the secure retention of records;
b) appropriate measures to safeguard IT systems; and
c) an appropriate security system.

27.2 The premises and its contents are insured (or there are alternative prompt methods of replacing lost items).

27.3 The provider has a Business Continuity Plan, which staff understand and can access, which will include both provision of premises and safeguarding/back up of records.

STANDARD 28 – Payment to carers

Underpinning legislation

Regulation 17 – Support, information and training for foster parents
Regulation 27 – Approval of foster parents
Schedule 5 – Matters and obligations in Foster Care Agreements

Outcome

Payments to foster carers are fair and paid in a timely way.
Foster carers are clear about the fostering service's payment structures and the payments due to them.

Standard

28.1 Each foster carer receives at least the national minimum allowance for the child, plus any necessary agreed expenses for the care, education and reasonable leisure interests of the child, including insurance, holidays, birthdays, school trips, religious festivals etc, which cover the full cost of caring for each child placed with her/him.

28.2 Payments of allowances and any fees paid are made promptly at the agreed time and foster carers are provided with a statement of payment at the end of each tax year.

28.3 Allowances and any fees paid are reviewed annually and the fostering service consults with foster carers in advance of any change to the allowance and fee.

28.4 The fostering service advises foster carers of financial and other support that is available to foster carers where a child remains with them after they reach the age of 18 or where they care for/provide a home for a child and their parent(s).

28.5 There is a clear and transparent written policy on payments to foster carers that sets out the criteria for calculating payments and distinguishes between the allowance paid and any fee paid. The policy includes policy on payment of allowances and any fee during a break in placement or should the fostering household be subject to an allegation.

28.6 The written policy and the current level of payments are provided annually to each foster carer and commissioners of the service. The foster carer receives clear information about the allowances and expenses payable, and how to access them, before a child is placed.

28.7 Criteria for calculating fees and allowances are applied equally to all foster carers, whether the foster carer is related to the child or unrelated, or the placement is short- or long-term.

28.8 Fostering service providers are clear about what equipment is being either loaned or given to foster carers.

28.9 Where a child is eligible for benefits as a result of a disability, foster carers are encouraged to apply for those benefits. There are regular recorded discussions about how any additional benefits are being spent to promote the best interests of the child.

STANDARD 29 - Notification of significant events

Underpinning legislation
Regulation 36 – Notifiable events
Schedule 7 – Events and notifications

Outcome
All significant events relating to the health and protection of children fostered by the service are notified by the registered person to the appropriate authorities.

Standard
29.1 The registered person has a system in place to notify, within 24 hours, persons and appropriate authorities of the occurrence of significant events in accordance with regulation 36. The system includes what to do where a notifiable event arises at the weekend.

29.2 A written record is kept which includes details of the action taken, and the outcome of any action or investigation, following a notifiable event.

29.3 The registered person has a system for notification to responsible authorities of any serious concerns about the emotional or mental health of a child, such that a mental health assessment would be requested under the Mental Health Act 1983.

29.4 Following an incident notifiable under regulation 36, the registered person contacts the responsible authority to discuss any further action that may need to be taken.

STANDARD 30 – Family and friends as foster carers

Underpinning legislation

Regulation 17 – Support, training and information for foster parents
CPPR 2010 – Regulations 24 and 25

Outcome

Family and friends foster carers receive the support they require to meet the needs of children placed with them.

Standard

30.1 The needs and circumstances of family and friends foster carers are taken into account when determining the fostering service's policies and practices.

30.2 The fostering service's Statement of Purpose includes the services and facilities that they provide to family and friends foster carers.

30.3 In deciding whether a relative, friend or other connected person should be approved as a foster carer, the decision maker takes into account the needs, wishes and feelings of the child and the capacity of the carer to meet these.

30.4 In seeking to support family and friends foster carers, the local authority fostering service works closely with the wider local authority children's services department, other departments, and agencies such as housing, to mitigate any limitations to the carer's capacity to care for a foster child.

30.5 When assessing an individual's suitability to be a family and friends foster carer, the likely length of the placement, the age of the child, the wishes and feelings and any concerns of the child and, if appropriate, the capacity of the wider family to contribute to the child's long term care, are taken into account.

30.6 Potential family and friends foster carers should be provided with information about the assessment process, so they know what is expected of them, how they will be assessed, including the criteria that will be used and how particular issues for family and friends foster carers will be addressed, and any support offered during the assessment process.

30.7 Family and friends foster carers are asked about their existing knowledge of the foster child's behaviour and background and any concerns they have about the child, as well as being provided with information about the child that is held by the fostering service.

30.8 The child's introduction to the new fostering arrangement takes account of the fact that, whilst the child may know the carer well, the carer's role in the child's life is now changing. This is explained to the child and the carer is provided with the support they need to manage this transition.

30.9 The fostering service takes into account the carer's, parents' and child's views about contact before the start of the placement, or as soon as possible afterwards, and puts in place appropriate supports to help manage contact.

30.10 Financial and other support is provided to all foster carers according to objective criteria that do not discriminate against foster carers who have a pre-existing relationship with the child. Family and friends foster carers may require some services to be delivered in a different way, but there should be equity of provision and entitlement.

30.11 Family and friends foster carers have access to training available to other foster carers, but the fostering service provider also offers training that addresses the particular needs and circumstances of family and friends foster carers.

30.12 Family and friends foster carers have access to support groups that meet their particular needs.

30.13 Supervising social workers who are supporting family and friends foster carers have training in the particular needs and circumstances of this group.

30.14 Where a family and friends foster carer is temporarily approved as a foster carer under regulation 24 of the Care Planning, Placement and Case Review (England) Regulations 2010, a full assessment is competed as soon as practicable, where the intention is for the child to stay with the carer, and always within the statutory timeframe set out in the regulations.

This standard only applies to local authority fostering services and those independent fostering services which approve family and friends foster carers. However, where family and friends are approved as foster carers the other standards apply as they do for other foster carers.

STANDARD 31 - Placement Plan and review

Underpinning legislation

Schedule 5 – Matters and obligations in foster care agreements
CPPR (2010):
Regulation 9 – Placement Plan
Part 6 – Reviews of the child's case

Outcome

Children are cared for in line with their Placement Plan/Short Break Care Plan.
The fostering service takes action to chase up outstanding reviews or visits from the responsible authority, contributes to those reviews and assists the child to contribute to their reviews.

Standard

31.1 The fostering service supports foster carers to play an active role in agreeing the contents of each child's placement plan, in conjunction with the responsible authority.

31.2 The foster carer is given a copy of the child's placement plan as soon as this is provided to them by the responsible authority. If provision of the care plan by the responsible authority is delayed, the fostering service follows this up with the responsible authority.

31.3 The foster carer is supported to contribute effectively to the review of their care plan, which includes the placement plan.

31.4 The foster carer is supported to assist the child to put forward their views, wishes and feelings as part of each review process, and the fostering service helps to ensure that these are fully taken into account by the child's responsible authority.

31.5 Foster carers are supported to explain the child's care plan, and any changes to those plans, to the child.

31.6 The fostering service contacts the responsible authority to request statutory reviews or visits if these are overdue for any child, or if a review has not already been arranged by the responsible authority and a change in the care plan is needed, there has been a significant change in arrangements for the child's care or a major action (e.g. a change of placement) which is not in the care plan appears likely.

31.7 The fostering service and foster carer contribute effectively to each child's Placement Plan review and statutory review of the child's care plan

31.8 Children are assisted to secure an independent advocate to support them in providing their views, wishes and feelings to statutory reviews.

Appendix 1: Source documents

Statutes

- Children Act 1989, Care Standards Act 2000, Adoption and Children Act 2002

Regulations

- Children Act 1989 Representations Procedure (England) Regulations 2006 SI 2006/1738
- Her Majesty's Chief Inspector of Education, Children's Services and Skills (Fees and Frequency of Inspections) (Children's Homes etc.) Regulations 2007 SI 2007/694
- Independent Review of Determinations (Adoption and Fostering) Regulations 2009 SI 2009/395
- The Care Standards Act 2000 (Registration) (England) Regulations 2010 SI 2010/2130
- Care Planning, Placement and Case Review (England) Regulations 2010 SI 2010/959
- Fostering Services (England) Regulations 2011 SI 2011/581
- Arrangements for Placement of Children by Voluntary Organisations and Others (England) Regulations 2011 SI 2011/582

Guidance

- Children Act 1989 Guidance and Regulations Volume 4: Fostering Services DFE-00023-2011
- Fostering Services: National Minimum Standards

Appendix 2: Further reading

CAE publications

Children Act Enterprises (CAE) publishes a series of guides on various aspects of the law pertaining to children. A full catalogue is available upon request from Children Act Enterprises, 103 Mayfield Road, South Croydon, Surrey CR2 0BH, tel: 020 8651 0554, fax: 020 8405 8483, email: childact@dial.pipex.com or they can be viewed on www.caeuk.org. Titles are as follows:

Children Act 1989 in the Context of the Human Rights Act 1998

Childminding and Day Care (England)

Child Protection

Residential Care of Children

Fostering

'How Old do I Have to be . . .?' (simple guide to the rights and responsibilities of 0–21-year-olds)

Domestic Violence (Part IV Family Law Act 1996 & Protection from Harassment Act 1997)

Looking After Children: Good Parenting, Good Outcomes (DH LAC System)

Crime and Disorder Act 1998

Sexual Offences Act 2003

Anti-Social Behaviour

Other useful books from BAAF

The New Fostering Standards, Regulations and Statutory Guidance: What's new? What's changed?, Nick Dunster, BAAF, 2011
A guide setting out a succinct outline of key themes and a comparative analysis of old and new standards and regulations, highlighting significant changes.

Adoption Now: Law, regulations, guidance and standards, Fergus Smith with Deborah Cullen, BAAF, 2011
A handy guide to adoption law in England and Wales.

Child Care Law: A summary of the law in England and Wales, Deborah Cullen and Mary Lane, BAAF, 2003
A guide to law pertaining to child care in England and Wales.

Fostering a Child, Henrietta Bond, BAAF, 2004
A unique introductory guide to foster care, including a full list of local authority and voluntary agencies.

Fostering: What it is and what it means, Shaila Shah, BAAF, 2003
A short, brightly illustrated children's guide to fostering, covering all the commonly asked questions.

Effective Fostering Panels, Sarah Borthwick and Jenifer Lord, BAAF, 2011
This guide offers good practice points to agencies in the operation of effective fostering panels.

Attachment, Trauma and Resilience, Kate Cairns, BAAF, 2002
A compelling account of the author's experience of fostering twelve children, including the research and practice implications for carers and professionals.

Fostering Attachments, Brian Cairns, BAAF, 2004
The author describes his experience of fostering twelve children, focusing on the practical lessons to be learnt by carers.

We are Fostering, Jean Camis, BAAF, 2003
A colourful workbook for birth children in foster families, including space for drawings and photographs.

What Happens in Court?, Hedi Argent and Mary Lane, BAAF, 2003
A user-friendly children's guide to help children understand the role a court might have in their lives.

All available from BAAF, Saffron House, 6–10 Kirby Street, London EC1N 8TS, telephone 020 7421 2604, email pubs.sales@baaf.org.uk, or visit www.baaf.org.uk.